THE SCOUTING JOURNEY

Clarke Green

Thanks Rob!

First Printing November, 2013

Cover design, text, and illustrations:

© 2013 by Clarke Green

All rights reserved. No part of this publication may be reproduced, distributed, or transmitted in any form or by any means, including photocopying, recording, or other electronic or mechanical methods, without the prior written permission of the publisher, except in the case of brief quotations embodied in critical reviews and certain other noncommercial uses permitted by copyright law.

Ordering Information:
Special discounts are available on quantity purchases by corporations, associations, and others. For details, contact the publisher, Clarke Green, at www.scoutmastercg.com

This book is not official publication of, nor is it endorsed by, the Boy Scouts of America or any other organization.

ISBN-13: 978-1492266822
ISBN-10: 1492266825

Scouter's families aren't ordinary, and they aren't married to ordinary people.

Ordinary husbands and wives go out to dinner at ordinary places where there are no speakers or programs or gangs of sugar-crazed Cub Scouts running around. Ordinary families share quiet evenings and weekends at home; they go on ordinary vacations.

Scouters do extraordinary things like spending a week at summer camp, going on weekend camp outs, and attending dozens of committee meetings.

Without an extraordinary wife, none of this would be possible. For her support and her love, I dedicate this book to my wife, Teddi.

Acknowledgements

None of this would be possible without the Scouts and Scouters who have so generously allowed me to be a part of their lives.

Scouting has been shaped by dedicated, concerned, caring people who have volunteered their time and resources to the movement over the past century. I readily acknowledge that their work, and their ideas have filtered through what I have read, heard, and seen to inform what I have written here.

I can't claim any ideas in this book are exclusively my own. In fact, I doubt many are original. If I have appropriated any ideas without attribution, it is purely by accident.

I am fortunate to have a sister, Deborah Green, who is also a supportive, dedicated, and talented editor. My deepest gratitude and love to Debbie.

Prologue

What is Scouting?

Not one in a hundred of our own people knows this.

Scouting is not a thing that can be taught by wording it in public speeches, nor by defining it in print. Its successful application depends entirely on the grasp of the Scout spirit ... a real understanding knowledge of the Scout ideals, the methods we use to gain them, and the reasons that underlie them. ...

Now these, you will say, are things that you know already, and don't need to be told. Yes, that is so. But what I want is that you should pass them on to those who don't know them.

— **Baden-Powell,** *B.P.'s Outlook*

Contents

Preface 1
Introduction 4
   A Perpetual Emergency? 4
   Scouting's Past 5
   Is Scouting Still Relevant? 9
A Joyously Impractical Journey 11
   Why Scouting? 12
   Why Me? 13
   Why Now? 15
   What You Need for the Journey 17
   What You Need in Your Head 17
   What You Need in Your Heart 18
The Map 24
   Our Destination — The Main Aim 24
   The Landscape of Scouting 26
   How We Travel — The Methods of Scouting 32
Our Travelling Companions 43
   The Scouts 43
   Parents 49
   Fellow Scouters 51
   Parent/Child — Scout/Scouter 53
The Scouter as Guide 56
   Two Types of Guides 56

- Three Types of leaders 57
- Techniques for Guiding Scouts 62
  - Practical Application of the Patrol System 62
  - Reflection 65
  - Guided Discovery 67
  - Inspiration 69
  - Mentoring 70
  - Positive Rites of Passage 71
- Learning by Challenge & Achievement 75
  - Step One — Learning by Doing 77
  - Step Two — Evaluation 78
  - Step Three — Reflection 80
  - Step Four — Recognition 82
- Youth Engagement 83
  - A Simple Formula 85
  - Real Responsibility 86
  - Inspiring Initiative 87
  - Observing from a Distance 89
  - Be Resilient 90
  - Finding the Advisor's Voice 91
  - Value the Discovery Process. 92
  - Citizenship and Leadership 93
- Outdoor Adventure 97
  - The Question of Scale 98

Outfitting 99
The Question of Risk 100
Risk and Age 102
Constructive Discipline 103
Appropriate Reactions to Bad Behavior 105
Applying Constructive Discipline 105
Consequences and Punishment 108
Positive Reinforcement 109
Lions, Tigers & Bears 111
Problem Scouters 111
Child Abuse and Neglect 113
What About Bullying? 115
Curing Homesickness 116
Bringing It All Together 118
Always Travelling; Never Arriving 122
References 125

Preface

In 1919, the founder of the Scouting movement, Robert Baden-Powell, published his vision of Scouting in a booklet titled *Aids to Scoutmastership*. Translated into many languages, often quoted, and frequently republished, this brief, unassuming little booklet remains a valuable link to the ideas that form the foundations of the Scouting movement. Unfortunately, Baden-Powell's century-old turns of phrase cloud these ideas for many modern readers. In the introduction to *Aids to Scoutmastership*, he writes:

> *You will find this book a disappointing one if you hope to find in it a set of definite stepping-stones to complete knowledge. I merely propose to state, as suggestive, the line which we have found to be successful, and the reasons for it.*
>
> *A man carries out suggestions the more wholeheartedly when he understands their aim.*
>
> *So most of these pages will be taken up with the objects of the steps rather than with the details of the steps themselves. These can be filled in by the learner according to his own ingenuity, and in harmony with the local conditions under which he is working.*
>
> — **Baden-Powell**, *Aids to Scoutmastership*.

See what I mean? It takes most of us a few careful passes to understand that quote.

2 / The Scouting Journey

What you are about to read is a sincere attempt to faithfully update Baden-Powell's vision for the present generation of Scouters. Like *Aids to Scoutmastership*, the result is not a systematic how-to guide; but a statement of the broad underlying concepts, the basic framework, of Scouting.

Over the last century, we Scouters have constructed a massive matrix of definitions, terms, and titles. Our jargon is helpful shorthand to the initiated; to others it is simply confusing. I've left out the jargon in an attempt to uncouple ideas from terminology that sometimes obscures them.

I use "Scouter" as a catchall title for any adult volunteer and "Scout" for youth members of any age. When the Scout oath is mentioned (some say promise, some say oath or promise) please infer "or promise."

"Patrol system" is one essential Scouting term with no suitable replacement. Where "patrol" is used, I mean any formally arranged small group of Scouts. This may be dens of cubs, crews of ventures, or any other designation given small groups. Some argue "patrol system" is incorrect, and we ought to say, "patrol method"—Baden-Powell used the terms interchangeably.

Most writing about Scouting over the past century has been aimed at boys and men. Since women and girls are equally important in Scouting, I have attempted to weed out gender-specific terms. Some quotes you'll read here are gender specific, but this is an artifact of the time they were written.

I am not a spokesperson for, nor have I obtained the endorsement of, any Scouting organization. There are hundreds of Scouting organizations around the world, each has their own particular way of doing things, but we all use the same basic map, or framework. Test what I have written against policies and procedures specific to your Scouting association (especially those concerning safety and youth protection).

My aim is creating a map to guide new Scouters as they begin their journey, and inspiring veteran Scouters to travel though familiar country with a fresh set of eyes.

Clarke Green

Introduction

A Perpetual Emergency?

Scouting was founded just over a century ago, in part, because some felt the next generation was in trouble. Youth were physically unfit, and disconnected from the natural world. They lacked spiritual consciousness; they were reluctant to involve themselves in the affairs of their community and nation. The next generation was spiraling out of control, trending toward immorality and dissipation.

Sounds familiar doesn't it? Has there ever been a time when we were not convinced the next generation was lost? This "perpetual emergency" may be just a trick of perspective. Once we are over the hill, we tend to lose sight of the trail we followed as we climbed to the top.

Naturally we Scouters are intent on helping the next generation form positive values—but Scouting is not just a hedge against the perilous future. It is a transformative journey following a guiding star: the Scout oath and law—a simple statement of virtues and obligations that have defined stable, enlightened societies throughout human history.

A century ago, the idea of Scouting took the world by storm, and continues on its transformative, joyous, journey today. Scouting is more than an alternative educational method or pleasant pastime. This movement, based on children's camping trips and activities, is much greater than it appears.

Scouting's Past

During his youth in Great Britain, Robert Baden-Powell had a keen interest in camping and woodcraft. As a military officer, he applied this knowledge to train his men to survive in the wilderness. While stationed in Africa, Baden-Powell befriended American born British officer Frederick Russell Burnham. Together they developed military scouting techniques that would become the basis of Baden-Powell's vision for the Scouting movement.

Baden-Powell rose to prominence late in the nineteenth century as a celebrated hero of the Boer War in the African Transvaal. When he returned home to England he learned a brief instruction book he authored to train soldiers—*Aids to Scouting*—had become a popular resource for teachers and youth leaders.

In July 1906, British-born Canadian-American author and illustrator Ernest Thompson Seton sent Baden-Powell a copy of his book for youth titled The Birch Bark Roll of the Woodcraft Indians. Later that year they met and discussed youth training programs. Drawing on his military experience and Seton's ideas, Baden-Powell conducted an experimental encampment of British boys on Brownsea Island off the coast of England in 1907.

The techniques and philosophy he employed on

Brownsea developed into his landmark book Scouting for Boys, an instant bestseller spawning a spontaneous worldwide youth movement.

Spurred by the tremendous reception Scouting for Boys received, Baden-Powell's initial aim to aid the youth of the United Kingdom expanded into nothing less than a vehicle for world peace.

> *Scouting was not a year old before other countries had formed their branches ... In twenty-one short years the Scout and Guide training has spread to forty-two different countries about the world, and has proved its potentiality as a factor in world peace.**

Not everyone embraced this spontaneous growth. Some urged Baden-Powell to patent his ideas before they got away from him. They feared his intentions would be diluted and even misdirected if Scouting was not centrally controlled. He probably sensed he could do little to control it had he wanted to!

The Scouting movement continued to spread. In 1920, in the devastating aftermath of World War I, Scouts traveled to the first World Jamboree in London. Baden-Powell called this gathering of recently warring nations with seemingly irreconcilable differences of politics, culture, and religion the "first great reunion of the world's boyhood."

As a military officer, Baden-Powell had not only witnessed the carnage of war first hand; he was intimately involved in its execution. Imagine how he must have felt surveying the Scouts gathered at that first world jamboree as the vision of Scouting's potential for fostering world peace unfolded before his eyes.

After ten days of camping and working together at the Jamboree the Scouts met with their founder and encouraged him to make this appeal:

Brother Scouts, I ask you to make a solemn choice. Differences exist between people of the world in thought and temperament.

The Jamboree has taught us that with mutual give and take under a common ideal, sympathy and harmony are established.

If it be your will, let us therefore endeavor to develop among our boys such comradeship through the world-wide Scout spirit of brotherhood that peace and goodwill may henceforth reign among men.

Are you willing to join in this high enterprise?*

The overwhelmingly positive response resulted in the formation of an International Scout Bureau. Thereafter, he bore the title his Scouts gave him, "The Chief Scout of the World." When he recalled this momentous occasion Baden-Powell quoted Bengali poet Rabindranath Tagore:

It is through brotherhood and not through organization that the world should be ordered... we are all citizens in the Kingdom of Ideas... there will be men large enough to see the human race as a whole, who understand that the good of the community as a family exists...*

Baden-Powell observed:

If we reflect that we members of the human family are only here on this earth together for a short span of life we realize that petty differences and fighting for little selfish ends are out of place in the Creator's scheme.*

Scouting simply, yet profoundly, asserts we can get along with each other if we try, we can make the world a better place.

Something as far-reaching as world peace begins with small things that concern a group of Scouts. Some want one thing for dinner; some want another. They discuss, debate, and arrive at an agreement. The everyday things Scouts do echo throughout their lives: "we can get along with each other if we try. We can make the world a better place."

Today the world movement of Scouting reaches past barriers of politics, socioeconomics, education, culture, and religion to serve youth in 170 countries. Scouts aim to bring peace, understanding, equality, service, and mutual respect to the world. When we volunteer our time to Scouting, we join a worldwide circle of people who share in this "high enterprise."

* **Baden-Powell,** *Scouting and Youth Movements*

Is Scouting Still Relevant?

Scouting is not a group of young people staging a continuous, historic re-enactment of the first Brownsea Island encampment. Today's Scouts preserve relevant traditions, but Scouting remains as dynamic and engaging as it was a century ago.

Baden-Powell was fond of pointing out that Scouting is not an organization: it is a movement. Movements are dynamic, and unpredictable. Scouts are independent and inventive; they think for themselves. When Scouts get hold of the dynamic ideas of Scouting, innovation and change are spontaneous.

Organizations tend to grow inflexible and arthritic; they struggle to contain this tremendous energy. If they don't renew themselves periodically, they risk losing the vital ideas that created them.

Renewal means change and not everyone finds change invigorating. What of our traditions? Haven't we always looked at the world this way? Why would we change now? Aren't we abandoning unchanging, timeless principles? The history of Scouting is, in large part, this tension between movement and organization.

Change does not mean we abandon ideas, traditions, and principles so much as learn more about what they mean. Today Scouts find the Scout oath and law embodies racial equality, gender equality, and religious pluralism; all ideas B.P may not have imagined or embraced when he wrote the oath and law a century ago.

Scouting's continued relevance really hinges on the attitude of each individual Scouter. We are always concerned about what is going to happen at the next meeting or camping trip. We strive to learn and follow rules and regulations, policies and procedures. We attempt to measure and quantify the progress of our Scouts. We have plenty of forms to fill in, records to maintain, and plans to develop.

All those practicalities are meaningless if we don't strive to grasp what is at the heart of the movement. We must learn the importance of the less practical, less tangible elements of Scouting. Scouting is not a manufacturing process aimed at producing a uniform product: it is a rambling journey that transforms lives. We don't ever reach a final destination, there's always another step to take, another challenge ahead.

1
A Joyously Impractical Journey

To travel hopefully is a better thing than to arrive, and the true success is to labor.

— *Robert Louis Stevenson,* Virginibus Puerisque

Scouting is an adventurous, transformative, and joyously impractical journey. "Scout" is a verb. Scouts reconnoiter, explore, discover, observe, experience, evaluate, advance, venture, and pioneer. Scouts experience life, rather than just studying life's possibilities.

Scouting is a transformative process, not a destination. We focus on where we are, rather than the next stop on the itinerary. We do not follow an easy road on a level grade or soften hard corners. Scouts revel in physical, mental, and spiritual challenges. Scouts aren't tourists; they are explorers committed to a journey of discovery, one step at a time, and one trail leading to the next, always moving forward.

Scouts find joy in things some people would call impractical. What practical person would voluntarily leave the hard-won comforts of home to traipse through the forest and sleep on the ground? What adult in their right mind would devote their precious free time to the intensity and joyful chaos of overseeing a group of Scouts?

I have shared a thousand campfires, camped, hiked, and canoed many miles; I've grown older—*perhaps* even wiser—in the company of Scouts and Scouters. As we covered literal trails through the wilderness, my Scouts were travelling the figurative trail toward adulthood.

I have seen Scouting's tremendous transformative potential at work, I know the trail, so let's get going! All you need to do is take that first step.

Why Scouting?

Why Scouting instead of sports or other youth groups, clubs, and teams? Other worthy pursuits for children do not form so much as reveal character. Scouting is aimed at forming character. Do you remember what it was like to be a child, how you yearned to grow up? Scouting is a framework that lends this yearning direction and structure.

We may look back on our own childhoods as bitter or sweet (more likely a combination of the two), but we may not fully recall the depth of feeling we experienced. We had our joyous, enlightening, empowering moments, and our doubtful, dark, and dangerous ones.

Every child's future is uncertain. Things can go well or tragically wrong. This is equally inspiring and terrifying for parents, especially during the often stormy, uncertain years of adolescence. Scouting does not shrink from the challenges of adolescence: it is built on them.

Nearly anywhere in the world, young people on the path to adulthood instinctively form groups, adopt uniforms, establish standards, develop a credo, and create initiatory challenges. The "uniform" may be torn jeans and black tee shirts, their standards and credo may be more directed at mayhem than order, and their initiatory challenges may be dangerous or anti-social.

Scouting does not ignore, battle with, or acquiesce to all this youthful energy—it offers direction and solace; it cooperates with the powerful forces at work. Scouting uses uniforms, standards of conduct, credos, and initiatory challenges to create an island of stability, a safe place to exercise independence, and discover positive values.

Why Me?

Why not you? Perhaps you doubt you are ideally suited to be Scouter, know enough to lead Scouts, or if the effort is worth your time. Every Scouter I have known has had to overcome those doubts so you are in good company!

Most of us start with an idealized picture of Scouting. When our ideal meets reality, we become disillusioned. *Disillusionment is actually a good thing*—we trade illusions for reality and begin making progress.

As a boy, I had a copy of the *Patrol Leader's Handbook* illustrated with drawings of perfect campsites, Scouts lined up neatly dressed in their uniforms, eager to listen to their patrol leader. My youthful attempts to organize our neighborhood gang did not even begin to resemble those idealized pictures.

We all have visions of perfection; we instinctively idolize ideal people, places, and things. Eventually we come to understand that perfection is a rare commodity. If we reject any solution short of perfection, we reduce reality to two black and white illusions. But reality is much more interesting, complex, and compelling than illusion!

Reality can be uncomfortable and challenging; the going can be tough. We have to bear with uncertainty and discomfort to push ahead to see what awaits us around the next bend. What awaits us may be bitter, or sweet—but we will never know unless we go. That uncertainty is the true joy of any journey!

Are you ready to get going? Maybe you are wondering:

Why Now?

Most of us volunteer as Scouters because our children are Scouts. I have never known a parent to regret spending time with their child as a Scouter. Some may regret they had not spent a great deal more.

My time with a child of my own in Scouting is now long past. Until you are in my shoes, you cannot know how fast those years slip by!

During the years adults serve as principal leaders for younger Scouts you'll share a lot of time with your child. As they grow up, adults step back and the Scouts themselves take on the principal leadership roles.

Sometimes, as our children grow older, circumstances strain the parent/child relationship. The opportunity to talk driving to or from a Scout meeting or preparing for a camping trip may be more meaningful than you imagine.

> **BE PREPARED!**
> It Goes By Fast
> We knew this day was coming, but it came way too fast. His mother and I were both in tears as we drove home after dropping him off at college. We were sad, proud, and somewhat surprised!
>
> In what seemed like a couple of months later, we were off to his graduation (how could four years pass so quickly?)
>
> His wedding day, our mad dash to the maternity ward, holding our new granddaughter, all seemed to happen in a few weeks.
>
> You have heard people say life goes by fast; the thing is you cannot really understand how fast until it happens to you!

Around the campfire or the meeting room, you learn other parents are experiencing the same challenges and triumphs. You lend perspective and support to each other when things are difficult. As you take refuge in the company of other parents, your child is taking refuge in the company of other Scouts.

Scouters get to see their children from a perspective few parents enjoy. We see them working with their peers, and with other adults. At the same time, our child watches us work with our peers, and other children.

A family who chooses Scouting chooses "all of the above." There are specific commitments of time and resources, but Scouting is not a closed system, it both encourages and requires active involvement in community, school, and family.

When the time comes for children to make their own way, Scouting helps ease the transition. Scouters have progressively let go and watched their children stand on their own two feet. They develop confidence in their children's abilities and reassurance that they are capable of making good choices. Because you shared Scouting, even decades later, you and your child have experiences in common that surpass the average parent/child relationship.

What You Need for the Journey

Go light, and the lighter the better so that you have the simplest material for health comfort and enjoyment.

— **Nessmuk**, *Camping and Woodcraft*

Good Scouters (like good travelers) tolerate adversity and uncertainty; they have a resilient, determined attitude, they travel light, travel smart, and go prepared.

Scouting needs folks who are willing to get going and keep going more than it needs experts or heroes. Just reading about the territory explained in this book isn't enough; you have to travel there to *know* the place. I can point out landmarks, and share the skills I've learned to travel well, but to become experienced yourself you have to get going and keep on going.

Don't be afraid of failing or getting lost. No matter how carefully we prepare something unexpected is bound to happen. Our plans fail now and again. There is always room for improvement; we may never have it all together! Be prepared to take on what comes, even if you aren't quite certain what that may be. Be patient with yourself, long-suffering with others, and cheerful when the going is difficult.

What You Need in Your Head

Good Scouters are learners with the good sense to apply what they learn. Do not wait to get started, or grow complacent once you have. Strive to know your role, ask questions, and get trained. Do not wait for knowledge to find you; seek it out.

- Take advantage of training courses.
- Familiarize yourself with the informational resources available from your Scouting organization.
- Learn from successes and failures. Have the humility to change if you get off course.
- Be open to new methods and ideas.
- Fulfill your role with appropriate gravity tempered by a sense of humor.

What You Need in Your Heart

Any worthwhile journey is a challenge of character and resolve. Scouters are generally big-hearted people, so you probably have plenty of character and resolve to start with!

Faith in Scouting

Anyone who has followed a set of directions, a map, or a recipe, has exercised exactly the kind of faith a Scouter needs. Have faith that Scouting can achieve what it claims

Scouters are not expected to blaze the trail, but to follow the map. Perhaps you have a healthy dose of skepticism, a strong personality, or are a little reluctant to follow directions. Follow the map anyway; rely on the trail blazed by Scouters who travelled through this landscape over the past century.

Personal Integrity

Be who you are, not some idealized concept of what you think a Scouter should be. Perhaps the finest example our Scouts can have is someone who struggles successfully against the same imperfections they encounter in themselves. Scouts are able to spot a hypocrite 100 yards away. They respect honest people in spite of their imperfections, but will not give the time of day to anyone pretending to be someone they are not.

Scouting is not a series of unpleasant lessons in a sugarcoating of camping and play. Scouts turn their noses up at the medicine concealed in the spoonful of sugar, so do not attempt to teach lessons. Simply allow the experiences of Scouting to unfold and Scouts will discover those lessons themselves.

A Vision for Scouts

> *A happy boy is a good boy, a good boy is a good citizen.*
> — **William Hillcourt**, *Scoutmaster's Handbook*

Everything in Scouting is designed to support the success and happiness of Scouts. Happiness is not the absence of difficulty. Happiness in Scouting comes from revealing the genuine joy of achievement, of taking the road less traveled, rather than the path of least resistance. Scouts don't want things to be easy; they love a challenge. They thrive on finding satisfaction and purpose in the things they do.

Compassion for Others and Yourself

If you want others to be happy, practice compassion. If you want to be happy, practice compassion.

— **The Dalai Lama,** The Art of Happiness

Compassion is an empathetic consciousness of others' distress coupled with a desire to alleviate it. Compassionate people look beyond themselves and strive always to "do unto others as you would have them do unto you."

Work flowing from a compassionate heart creates its own energy. As we work to make other people's lives better, our own lives become richer and happier.

Patience and Persistence

I admire people who are not easily upset, frustrated, or irritated; who can be calm, composed, and levelheaded even when things are difficult.

Someday I may be one of those people! Until then, I just have to continue to take a deep breath, count to ten, or step away for few moments to regain control and perspective. Sometimes I find myself concentrating on the one wrong thing in a landscape of success. I worry about what didn't happen or what is about to happen, and miss what is happening right now.

Working with young people may be invigorating, but it is also exasperating at times. Their energy and willingness to learn can be equaled or surpassed by indecisiveness and stubbornness.

Scouters need patience and persistence to tolerate adversity and uncertainty. Our journey is not designed to be easy or comfortable. We may feel we are paddling against the stream, but even so, we keep on paddling.

During the Nazi occupation of Poland during World War II, the Polish Scouting movement went underground. Poles fleeing the communist government that followed took their Scouting traditions with them. The Polish Scouting movement in exile remained strong and held quadrennial world Jamborees.

In 1988, thousands travelled from all over the world to our local Scout camp for one of these Jamborees. There I met a man in is eighties who, as a Scoutmaster during the Nazi occupation, led his Scouts to be saboteurs blowing up railways and bridges in the resistance. I met people who had established Scout troops in the ghettos, who showed me the tattoos of the concentration camps where they kept Scouting alive in unbelievable circumstances.

Our challenges fade in comparison to the difficulties these brave Scouters endured. Certainly, we can withstand the comparatively small conflicts and discomforts we are likely to encounter.

Chutzpah

Chutzpah (pronounced *hoots'-pah*) is a Yiddish word meaning a combination of gall, nerve, guts, and presumption with a tinge of arrogance. Scouters all need a little chutzpah.

We need to stand up for our Scouts, for ourselves and for the ideas essential to Scouting. It takes chutzpah not only to try new ideas and methods, but also to stick to proven ones.

It takes chutzpah to be a Scout, to stand out, to achieve in a world that sometimes belittles anyone who dares to explore his or her own potential.

A Love of the Outdoors

The outdoors is par excellence the school for observation and for realizing the wonders of a wondrous universe.

— **Baden-Powell**, Aids to Scoutmastership

Scouters are at home in the outdoors. Their love of outdoor life sparks energy and enthusiasm even when circumstances are difficult.

They help Scouts discover the greater messages of outdoor life, self-sufficiency, the fragility and power of nature, and our role as stewards of the natural world

Gathering sticks to light a fire in a circle of stones. Turning your face to the fire, your back on the night: feeling the sharpness of the cold, the weight of the heat. Being soaked by rain and warmed by the sun. All are precious opportunities to explore how we relate to the natural world and to each other.

A Child's Perspective

The scoutmaster guides the boy in the spirit of an older brother. He must have the boy spirit in him; and must

be able to place himself on a right plane with his boys as a first step.

— **Baden-Powell,** Aids to Scoutmastership

Do you remember what it was like to be a child? Scouters are able to see things from a child's perspective, to understand and share a child's curiosity, energy, and ambition.

Using this perspective, we create active opportunities for our Scouts to explore and achieve. We treat Scouts as individuals rather than just another head in the herd. We strive to see things from their point of view and guide them forward in the spirit of an older brother or sister.

2
The Map

Scouting organizations apply the general philosophy of the Scouting in specific policies, procedures, and activities. These specifics define a program, and that program is our map. Scouters who haven't studied the program map may find they miss important signposts, or go off course with no idea how to get back on track.

It's not my intention to describe the details of a single Scouting organization's programs, let alone those of all the various worldwide organizations. Each has their own specific way of doing things, but all share common methods aimed at a common goal.

Every Scouter needs to understand our common goal and the methods we employ to reach that goal. Once we've understood these things, we know where are we headed, the landscape we are travelling through, and how we travel forward.

Our Destination — The Main Aim

Our aim is to produce healthy, happy, helpful citizens; to eradicate the prevailing narrow self-interest;

personal, political, sectarian and national, and to substitute for it a broader spirit of self-sacrifice and service in the cause of humanity; and thus to develop mutual goodwill and cooperation not only within our own country but abroad, between all countries.

— **Baden-Powell,** Aids to Scoutmastership

Scout organizations have their own distinct mission statements, declarations of principle, credos, and definitions. All agree, generally, that Scouting's "main aim" is:

To encourage physical, intellectual, emotional, social, spiritual and character growth in young people enabling them to take a constructive role in their local, national and international community.

Where are the skills, achievements, and awards most of us associate with the goals of Scouting? Those tangible results may indicate we've hit the mark, but they are only incidental, we are aimed at greater things.

Years ago I served as a Scout camp archery director and learned how seemingly insignificant things affect the flight of an arrow. Aiming is more than pointing at the target and hoping for the best.

When I asked one experienced archer about aiming technique I was told to concentrate on an X printed on the center of the paper target that was barely half an inch high! The archer told me he didn't have to see the X, he knew it was there and pictured it in his mind as he aimed.

Scouters need to know the seemingly insignificant things that affect the trajectory of our Scouts. We need to understand the main aim and, just as the archer did, hold that vision in our minds.

Good Scouters prioritize everything they do against achieving the main aim. Everything worth doing has to do with our Scout's progress. If we find what we are aren't travelling toward the main aim we stop, and get back on track!

The Landscape of Scouting

Why does a boy or girl decide to become a Scout? They'll tell you that they want to have fun, to spend time with their friends—from a Scout's perspective, it's usually just that simple.

We know there's more to it than that. What Scouts experience as "fun" are actually significant developmental opportunities. Scouts can expect to experience these things:

Physical Development
Scouts go camping and take part in adventurous activities in the outdoors. They play games, and are always on the move.

Emotional Development
The Oath and Law come alive in activities designed to require interaction, cooperation, and looking out for each other.

Intellectual Development
Scouts learn practical skills and explore careers through a system of awards and recognitions.

Social Development
Scouting cooperates with family and community to offer opportunities that shape Scouts into contributing members of society.

Character Development
Scouting is driven by strong ethical and moral imperatives that aid Scouts in forming an internal standard of character and conduct.

Spiritual Realization
Scouting provides opportunities to understand one's spiritual reality and learn to respect the spiritual choices of others.

Just how we shape experiences to fulfill these promises is important. Scouters aren't just another teacher, coach, or activity leader. Teachers, coaches, and youth leaders do great work; but the Scouter's role is different.

Scouting shares similarities with other youth activities, but no other program is exactly like it. There are some important distinctions:

Scouting is:	Scouting is not:
Educational	An academic system of schooling
Something Scouts do for themselves	Something adults do for them
Something we do with our children	Exclusively parent/child time
A series of attainable challenges	A system of measurement
A challenging, enriching activity	Childcare or baby-sitting
A planned activity	An all-or-nothing commitment
An outdoor program	A series of classes or meetings
Age-appropriate activities	A "one size fits all" program
Fun with a purpose	Entertaining distractions
Moral principles and ethical actions	An ideology of conformity

Scouting Educates

Scouting educates, but not in the academic sense. Scouts do learn, but what they learn is not an end in itself. Moral and ethical imperatives are woven into every activity.

Throughout this book, I tease out the different threads of this educational fabric but, as an old preacher once said, "it's a tanglement." One thread pulls on another, they cross, uncross, and loop back on themselves to form a system of education unlike any other.

Scouting is a Game

Scoutmasters must necessarily be above petty personal feeling, and must be large-minded enough to subject

> *their own personal views to the higher policy of the whole. Theirs is to teach their boys to "play the game,"*
>
> — **Baden-Powell**, Aids to Scoutmastership

"The higher policy of the whole," or the rules of the game, are crucially important. Rules are not optional; rules create the game.

Rules are not there to spoil our fun or slow us down. Scouting's "rules"—the specifics of the program—define Scouting just as rules define a sport like basketball.

If the goal of playing basketball was limited to passing a ball through a hoop as often as possible, we would be tempted to change the rules. Why dribble the ball when carrying it is much more efficient? Why have the hoops so small and up so high? Why restrict the area of play or the number of players? We could score many more points if we changed the rules; but we would no longer be playing the game of basketball.

The game of basketball is more than getting a ball through a hoop and Scouting is much more than earning badges or learning skills. If the aim of Scouting were earning badges, we would put our energy into making it possible for Scouts to earn lots of badges. If it were just learning skills, we would concentrate on educating Scouts as thoroughly as possible.

A good basketball coach works within the construct of the rules of basketball. A good Scouter understands there is a similar construct to Scouting and works within those rules.

Coaches never leave the sidelines to play the game and neither do Scouters. The sidelines in Scouting can be hard to find. After all, they are not painted on the floor or chalked on a field. We are not players; our role is enabling Scouts to play the game.

Scouting is Cooperative

How do we compete for a Scout's attention when there are so many competing activities to choose from? Scouting does not begin and end at the threshold of the meeting room or gateway of the campsite. Scouts are full participants in their community, school, and family.

Unfortunatley some youth groups or teams demand nothing short of perfect attendance. We may think this forces Scouts to make an "either/or" decision, but that is not the case.

When our Scouts miss meetings or activities because they are involved in sports, a school club, or a church group we encourage them to carry what they have learned as a Scout with them. If Scouting becomes an either/or decision, our Scouts lose the opportunity to exercise the oath and law in their wider community.

Scouting does not compete with other things young people do; it cooperates with them.

Scouting is Age Appropriate

Scouting is not a "to do" list of activities to check off as quickly as possible. Scouts take on challenges and progress through the program at a rate appropriate to their age.

Do not push or drag Scouts into the next challenge before they have had the chance to experience the last one. Scouts who are rushed along may miss important milestones. Even if you think your Scouts are prodigies and ought to jump ahead to more challenging activities, stay with the program.

Scouting is Inclusive

The transformative power of Scouting is aimed at making us all useful, engaged, compassionate human beings. Scouting is an open invitation for growth and adventure, not an exclusive, special society for the worthy. Excluding young people from Scouting because we consider them somehow unworthy is inimical to the principles of the Scout oath and law.

The foundational principles of Scouting are strong because they find broad acceptance and influence in every corner of the world. We should eliminate discriminatory barriers in our own minds and hearts and welcome all who make a commitment to achieving the aims of Scouting.

How We Travel — The Methods of Scouting

Now shall I walk, or shall I ride? "Ride," Pleasure said; "Walk," Joy replied.

— **W.H. Davies,** *The Collected Poems*

Once we know where we are headed and the landscape we are passing through, it's time to look at exactly how we travel. Our journey is an adventurous ramble, a pilgrimage, whose greatest joy is in the trip itself. The methods of Scouting set our pace. We aren't flying over the territory; we are traipsing through it, taking in all the voyage has to offer.

Scouting has a number of methods that move us along like the muscles and tendons attached to our bones interact so we can walk. Outdoor adventures and the patrol system are the bones—without them, we can't move forward.

Outdoor Adventure

I cannot impress on Scoutmasters too highly the value of the camp in the training of Scouts; in fact, I think that its whole essence hangs on this.

— **Baden-Powell,** *Aids to Scoutmastership*

Everything we do is aimed at getting Scouts outdoors. Scouting becomes just another club if it stays inside. The skills learned and practiced in the meeting room are meaningless if they are not put into action in the campsite.

Aside from the obvious practical skills of camping and trekking outdoor adventure demands Scouts share responsibilities and learn to live with one another. They find a thousand different experiences for growth working within the dynamics of their patrol.

The Patrol System

> *The Patrol System is the one essential feature in which Scout training differs from that of all other organizations, and where the System is properly applied, it is absolutely bound to bring success. It cannot help itself!*
>
> — **Baden-Powell**, Aids to Scoutmastership

In my attempt to avoid organizational Scouting jargon, I found no alternative for the term "patrol system'" because nothing else is remotely like this *"one essential feature."* If we are not applying the patrol system, we are not Scouting.

The central importance of the patrol system prioritizes everything. This book, (or nearly any book about Scouting for that matter), could accurately be titled "How to Apply the Patrol System." All of the advice I have to share converges on this deceptively simple, often underplayed, sometimes ignored, method of Scouting.

Don't get stuck on the term "patrol"; any small group of Scouts (from a Scouts Australia "Joey Mob," to a Boy Scouts of America "Venture Crew") is built on the principles of the patrol system.

The patrol system is a model democracy. Every large group is divided into smaller self-governing groups with leaders who represent them to a decision-making body of small-group leaders.

The patrol system develops the ideals of active citizenship (self-control, mutual respect, team spirit and character) by balancing personal responsibility, respect for authority, and group responsibility. A spirit of friendly competition among patrols raises the efforts of individual Scouts, the patrol, and the larger group.

It's that simple, but don't be misled—understanding the practicalities of the patrol system, and making sure it is *"properly applied"* is not easy. It only takes a few words to describe golf, but any golfer knows it takes a lifetime to master the game.

Focus thoroughly and unfailingly on putting the patrol system into practice. I have laid out how to do this in the chapter titled *Techniques for Guiding Scouts*. To belabor the point—this is not an optional feature; it is *"the one essential feature," "…it is absolutely bound to bring success. It cannot help itself!"*

A Moral Code for Ethical Action

Ideals are like stars: you will not succeed in touching them with your hands, but like the seafaring man on the ocean desert of waters, you choose them as your guides, and following them, you reach your destiny.

— **Carl Schurz,** *Speech at Faneuil Hall, Boston, 1859*

The Scout oath or promise and law are aspirational, affirmative statements that inspire and encourage us forward; a moral code embodying virtues valued throughout human history.

Baden-Powell's original promise and law are the basis for the different versions of the Scout oath and law adopted by Scouting organizations all over the world:

The Scout Oath or Promise

On my honor, I promise that I will do my best—
To do my duty to God and the King (or to God and my Country).
To help other people at all times and to obey the Scout Law.

The Scout Law

A Scout's honor is to be trusted.
A Scout is loyal.
A Scout's duty is to be useful and to help others.
A Scout is a friend to all and a brother to every other Scout.
A Scout is courteous.
A Scout is a friend to animals.
A Scout obeys orders of his parents, Patrol Leader or Scoutmaster without question.
A Scout smiles and whistles under all difficulties.
A Scout is thrifty.
A Scout is clean in thought, word and deed.

Everything Scouts do and how they do it springs from the oath and law, what Baden-Powell called our "binding disciplinary force."

Service to Others

Scouting is not an inward-facing movement. Service freely given to our communities is a key part of Scouting and of good citizenship.

Baden-Powell established the Scout motto: "do a good turn daily" to help Scouts learn to look beyond their own interests to the interests of others. Working for the good of others has a reciprocal effect benefiting both those who serve and those being served. A sense of brisk, energetic, and ready service builds character.

Scouts of all ages should be encouraged to individual acts of service, as should the larger group. Scouter's who make service an integral part of their planning reap many benefits for their Scouts and for their community.

Spiritual Development

It is not the slightest use to preach the Scout Law or to give it out as orders to a crowd of boys: each mind requires its special exposition of them and the ambition to carry them out.

— **Baden-Powell,** Aids to Scoutmastership

Scouting is aimed at bringing people together in fellowship rather than separating them. Scouting encourages spirituality, but has no dogma, does not advocate a specific form of religious observance, nor is it a religious system. Scouts express their personal convictions without aggressiveness, overcome prejudices, and show respect for different faiths.

What, then, does the Scout oath's pledge to "do my duty to God" mean? Scouting offers no objective test. It is incumbent on individual Scouts to observe this duty according to their own conscience, teaching, and tradition. Most young people develop an adult approach to spirituality, religion, and faith only after challenging and questioning their religious heritage.

Scouting's spiritual fabric is woven from the common threads of humanity to inspire reverence for the best and highest in us all. When we take the hand of a fellow Scout, we transcend the constructs of religion to something deeper and broader—an elemental, indefinable, common point where we stand as brothers and sisters.

Exploring nature in our outdoor activities, building relationships, showing compassion, sharing, co-operating with—and serving—others are all powerful opportunities for spiritual development.

We use the experiences of Scouting to help young people discover and incorporate spiritual meaning in their lives. We don't achieve this through rote religious instruction, or inserting religious observances onto Scout activities. We find reflective moments that help Scouts link their Scouting experiences to their specific spiritual and religious heritage. We illuminate these experiences with the meaning of the Scout Oath and Law.

Individual Growth

A measure of individual growth results from the acquisition of skills and recognition in the advancement program. However, we cannot be reminded often enough: the skills and badges Scouts acquire have an ulterior motive.

Individual growth happens in a group of equals actually living out the oath and law in cooperation and reciprocity with other Scouts. These interactions make the oath and law living realities, rather than lifeless concepts preached by adults.

Association with Adults

While Scouts benefit from the example Scouters provide, there is more to our role than simply modeling behavior. In the interest of education, our children spend their formative years in schools where the ratio of children to adults weakens useful adult association. This isolation foments a youth culture distinct from the adult world.

For centuries, puberty marked both the cultural and biological transition between childhood and adulthood. Today longer life spans and a longer period of education have separated the cultural transition to adulthood from the biological transition of puberty. Today we consider someone has reached adulthood many years later than we did only a century ago.

With all its advances and benefits in modern society often leaves children to navigate their adolescent years with little meaningful adult influence. By associating with adults in Scouting, young people get a broader adult perspective of the world. Adults with sincere interest in young people's well-being can make a profound difference. Meaningful collaboration with adults moderates the excesses and avoids the pitfalls common to those awkward years between adolescence and adulthood.

Uniform

A like uniform hides all differences of social standing in a country and makes for equality; but, more important still, it covers differences of country and race and creed, and makes all feel that they are members with one another of the one great brotherhood.

— **Baden-Powell,** *27 Years with Baden-Powell*

"Uniform" is an adjective as well as a noun. Uniforms are equalizing, they represent that what we share is of greater importance than the ways that we differ. Uniforms are a practical expression of our commitment to Scouting and our membership in a worldwide movement. Wearing the uniform correctly and neatly is a sign that we value being associated with what Scouting represents.

A uniform is also a travelogue of each individual Scout's journey. Badges and patches show where we have been and what we have done.

It is human nature to associate a person's identity with what they wear. There's a little part of every rugged individual that resists being "uniform," and some people shy away from the strong visual statement made by wearing a uniform. Some Scouts may find the idea of wearing a uniform difficult to reconcile with their own vision of themselves. What young people wear (or don't wear) has always caused the older generation agitation.

Of course, we know that who is inside the uniform is infinitely more important than the uniform itself. There is no stronger way to encourage good uniforming in Scouts than the example set by Scouters. Achievements and positions of responsibility displayed on the uniform

BE PREPARED!
Scouts are not Soldiers

During the early years of the movement, arguments were made for and against militarism in Scouting. Our founder, (a career military man), did not intend Scouting to be a military organization.

Many active and veteran service members volunteer as Scouters. Anything that blurs the distinction between military practices and Scouting ought to be avoided.

Scouting's hierarchical authority structure isn't a military equivalent.

Discipline is not applied with militaristic fervor.

Scout uniforms should not encroach on military similarity.

Anyone attending a camping trip with my Scouts would admire how well we follow Baden-Powell's lead; there's little about them that looks like regimentation or militaristic discipline!

are not indicative of a strict authoritarian structure, so much as a guide to who is who.

Progressive System of Challenges

Scouting's progressive system of challenges is commonly called advancement. By completing a number of specific requirements, Scouts advance in rank or status signified by badges or patches.

Earning badges is great fun for Scouts, but there is a much more important process at work. If we are sidetracked by the mechanics, we miss the intention of advancement.

Ceremony

A ceremony is a book in which a great deal is written.

— *George I. Gurdjieff,* In Search of the Miraculous

Saluting, lowering and folding a flag with respect, and a sense of moment leaves a greater impression than listening to a lecture on patriotism. Opening a meeting with the recitation of the Scout oath and law promotes discipline better than posting rules of conduct on the wall. The formal public presentation and recognition of a Scout's achievement tells the story of a meaningful milestone.

Ceremony is a time to reflect, to stop, listen, and share the importance of a moment, to consider our values and aspirations. Scouting ceremonies are best when they are meaningful, direct, and brief without being staid or flowery. Sincerity is the most important production value; the tone is formal, but short of overblown theatrics.

3
Our Travelling Companions

As a Scouter, I have worked with people from every part of the political, socio-economic, educational, and religious spectrum. I've seen the great unifying potential of Scouting at work as we labor together in an atmosphere of mutual respect. Scouting an enriching experience where I have formed decades-long friendships and broadened my own horizons.

All Scouters ought to strive to better know their Scouts, the Scouts' families, and fellow Scouters. The experiences and relationships change both us and the Scouts and Scouters we are working with.

The Scouts

The most important volunteers in Scouting have more power and influence than the highest official. Without their participation, Scouting would come to a complete halt. They bring endless energy, resources, and real transformational power to their role. They are the only volunteers we simply cannot afford to lose.

The single most important volunteers in Scouting are the Scouts themselves. Scouts make a voluntary decision to participate and we Scouters have our positions only to serve the interests and goals of the Scouts.

Scouts depend on consistent people, relationships, and experiences. They should be confident that their safety, happiness, and peace of mind are important to us. Even the most self-assured Scouts question their own abilities and need expressions of affirmation and confidence.

Scouts are testing boundaries more out of curiosity than willful disobedience. Although they question rules and push limits, they actually appreciate (often begrudgingly) boundaries that define what is expected of them

Stages of Development

Scouting programs have age divisions corresponding to basic stages of development. The next pages sketch a broad overview of three basic developmental stages.

Understanding the general characteristics of the age group we are serving helps shape our response.

Middle Childhood 5-9 Years

General Characteristics:	Our Response:
Vigorous, full of energy, generally restless.	Balance high-energy activities and quiet activities.
Want all of everything, finds making choices difficult. Unpredictable preferences and strong refusals.	Build confidence in their ability to make decisions, help them set individual goals
May blame others for anything that goes wrong.	Give lots of positive attention and let them help define the rules. Ask questions to develop problem-solving skills.
May fool around, whisper, or bother other children.	Pick focused times to talk without distractions.
Find it difficult to accept criticism, blame, or punishment.	Help them learn from criticism. Ask, "how could you do that differently next time?"
May be self-centered and boastful.	Help them negotiate social relationships.
.Must be a winner; changes rules to fit own needs; may have no group loyalty. If not the winner, often accuses others of cheating.	Encourage non-competitive games and activities.
Very concerned with personal behavior, particularly as it affects family and friends; sometimes blames others for own wrongdoing.	Talk about and encourage self-control, making good decisions.

Pre-Teens 9-13 Years

General Characteristics	Our Response...
Self-conscious, feel as if others are judging them; believe no one can relate to their experiences.	Encourage sharing ideas and feelings in reflection. Listen carefully. Be sensitive to teasing; it can cause serious problems.
Beginning to understand how one person can influence others.	Guide influence toward positive ends; model good behavior and values.
Does assess risk, but tends to give more weight to potential rewards than to negative consequences.	Monitor potentially risky situations; explain the consequences of choices.
Overwhelmingly concerned with winning the approval of peers and social acceptance.	Encourage acceptance and understanding of differences.
Better able to think about the future and to consider multiple possibilities at once.	Help exercise this developing skill in progressive responsibilities.
May make abrupt changes of behavior.	Some changes are positive, some are not. Be alert and seek help.
Concerned with asserting independence and defining relation to authority.	Maintain consistent, fair boundaries. Exercise authority judiciously.

Young Adults 14-18 Years

General Characteristics	Our Response...
Better able to understand other points of view. Increased sense of personal beliefs. Strong convictions regarding social and political change.	Encouraging reflection and discussion, promote the ideas of tolerance and mutual respect.
Uses expanding intellect to logically challenge authority. Tension and conflict from increased assertion of independence	Patience with challenges, understanding these are to be expected, reacting appropriately.
Less influenced by peer pressure, more likely to seek knowledge independently. Increased sense of vocation.	Provide broad opportunities for activities that leverage these interests.

Differences and Disabilities

Scouting is a broadening, enriching experience for anyone with developmental or physical differences and the "normal" Scouts and Scouters (if there is such a thing!) who work with them.

Scouting is a safe haven for learning to live and work with just about anyone. Thankfully, in recent decades, we have gained more understanding of, and sensitivity to, differences and disabilities.

Differences, as you may expect, are simply ways people are not the same. For example, some of us are cognitively different. We are not *incapable*, we simply relate to the world differently. What seems irrational or odd to one is perfectly rational and normal to another. Differences are not irrational or wrong; they are just different!

Disabilities, however, make it difficult or impossible for someone to do the things other people do. Some years ago, a family relocating to our area brought their two sons (the older brother had Down Syndrome) to our Scout Troop. I was worried. Would we have to make special arrangements? How would other parents react? Remembering how cruel we had been as children to anyone we felt wasn't "normal" I was concerned how our Scouts would react.

I shouldn't have worried. Our Scouts immediately accepted both brothers as their own. This revelation helped me look at the world differently, cultivate patience and tolerance, and honor every person's own unique nature.

Scouts who come to us with differences or disabilities are likely to have professionally determined diagnoses and follow a regimen of treatment or special help at school and at home. Special educational plans used in schools do not always work, nor are they always the best path to follow in the context of Scouting.

Schools use results-oriented measurements that simply do not apply to the things Scouts do. Both children and parents may find that the best plan for Scouts with differences and disabilities is actually taking little notice of them. I am not suggesting we be callous or indifferent, but that we allow plenty of room for Scouts to help each other solve whatever challenges they encounter. Unlike school, keeping up or getting ahead is not the goal. Scouts work together and only get ahead individually when they are all making progress.

Many of my Scouts have been on the spectrum of learning differences and disorders. In most cases, when we work with their particular abilities rather than trying to account for their disabilities, they sail right along with their fellow Scouts. Scouts who learn faster, are more sociable, or better physically abled apply those talents to help their fellow Scouts.

I want to emphasize that I am not suggesting we deny assistance where it is needed, or take special measures when warranted. I only want to point out the powerful potential that comes from Scouts working together and helping each other—something that is not usually a component of standard educational plans.

Parents

We work hand-in-hand with parents to help our Scouts become active, contributing, loyal members of their families. Rather than trying to explain Scouting to them, listen to their expectations carefully and you will hear familiar themes. These shared expectations are the basis for our partnership.

Regular interaction with parents to share plans and promote participation strengthens the partnership. We expect most parents to experience a level of discomfort entrusting the care of their child to others. Parents advocate the best interests of their child to the best of their ability. This advocacy takes all forms. Parents may express themselves in positive or negative ways. Whatever their state of mind, our response to parents is polite, measured, and professional (even volunteers need a sense of professionalism about our work).

Family Environments

Each family creates its own individual environment so we must be prepared to work with different family standards and expectations. A Scout's home environment may be supportive or it may be negative. We do our best to make a Scout's experience positive, regardless of the level of support we receive, or negative influences we must overcome.

How we were raised and how we chose to raise our children are not the only "right" ways. Even if we disapprove of a Scouts' home environments, we respect the wishes of their families. Looking into another's home is like looking into the mechanism of an old pocket watch. We see things spinning and clicking, but have little knowledge of exactly what's going on. Tinkering with a watch movement, or someone's family, without the requisite skills and knowledge is never a good idea.

Family Problems

Every family encounters problems from time to time. Some problems are transient; some are permanent. We do our best to keep these problems from negatively affecting a Scout's experience. Scouting may the only refuge a child has from family troubles. We accept our Scouts as they are despite influences they have to deal with at home. Should actual abuse or endangerment come to light it's incumbent on us to respond according to local laws (this is discussed in more detail in chapter 10.)

Fellow Scouters

Some of my best and oldest friends are Scouters. People who volunteer their time on behalf of others are some of the most wonderful people I have met.

There are differences and high emotions from time to time, but a little goodwill, perspective, and a sense of humor goes a long way. Tension and difficulties among Scouters is nothing new. During the first decade of Scouting Baden-Powell wrote in his column for *The Scouter* magazine:

> *...it is almost beyond belief that grown-up, or nearly grown-up, men can take little matters so seriously and so narrowly as some of them do. If they had only a sense of humor, or had a slightly wider range of view, so that they could see the other side of the question or its greater aim, they, too, would smile at the littleness of it all.*

Scouters, as a rule, are willing to pitch in and help; there's always plenty to do! Every single volunteer committee and organizational chart seems to have a perpetual vacancy. The combination of willing, helpful people, and numberless unfilled positions, makes becoming over-committed all too easy. Beware of over-extending yourself; volunteers who take on too much suffer from burn out, and we often lose them altogether.

My advice to new Scouters is to focus on one role. Become expert in it through training, study, and experience. Take on additional responsibilities only after giving due consideration to the demands involved.

Some Scouters who take on key roles tend to stay in them. I have been a Scoutmaster for almost 30 years. It comes to mind, though, that staying in this role for so

BE PREPARED!
The "Old Guard"

Some long-serving Scouters (The "Old Guard") want to tell you how it used to be, and why the way we do it now is wrong.

A long record of service does not mean any Scouter is particularly wise, knowledgeable, or necessarily correct about anything.

I have been around long enough to be in the Old Guard. Some of us cannot remember being younger and more energetic. We can give you many reasons against new ideas.

Do not take what the Old Guard (including me!) says as gospel. Test every theory, every practice, and every bit of advice you are given. Check the resources your Scouting organization provides.

The final authority is not the Old Guard, it is the program.

long may have denied other worthy Scouters the experience. While I have no regrets, given the chance to do it all again I may not have occupied the same role for quite so long in order to create an opportunity for others.

The world at large and Scouting in particular needs both bounding, energetic game-changers and older folks with knowledge grounded in years of experience. There will always be some tension between the two. It is incumbent on the older folks to strike the balance, respond, and not dismiss—to help realize the potential of new energy and enthusiasm.

Parent/Child — Scout/Scouter

The dual role of being a Scouter and parent of a Scout is a challenge that is easily outweighed by the rewards. A good parent and a good Scouter share similar goals, but Scouters should not impose the same expectations or authority we have for our own children on our Scouts. On average, parents are more demanding, critical, and emotional when working with their own child.

Things go much smoother when we prepare our children and ourselves to observe the boundary between these two roles. You may do and say things as a Scouter that make your children proud. You may do and say some things that make them cringe. They will, no doubt, return the favor.

Your child's reasons for being a Scout are different from your reasons for being a Scouter. You want to spend time with your child; they are almost always more interested in spending time with their friends.

Parents and children have "inside information" that can skew a Scouter's judgment and objectivity. They know what goes on at home, school, and work; they know each other's history, strengths, and weaknesses. I've found having a trusted fellow Scouter who you can talk to frankly goes a long way to balancing the roles of parent and Scouter. Of course, you can return the favor by helping them in the same way.

As you balance the roles of parent and Scouter, your child balances the roles of child and Scout. Discuss this with your child, agree on some boundaries, and do not switch roles too often. Do not treat your child as a child one minute and a Scout the next. Explain they need to accept the same responsibility as other Scouts and you cannot be expected to treat them differently.

At times, especially with younger Scouts, they need some consolation or help only a parent can offer. It may help to set aside time within a Scouting activity when you spend time as a parent with your child. Walk away from the group, address any concerns, share your thoughts with one another, and then return to the Scouter, Scout role.

Should I make My Child Stay in Scouts?

Childhood likes and dislikes change quickly—sometimes from hour to hour! Children who lose interest in Scouting one day may change their minds the next, but they may also have reached an impasse.

> **BE PREPARED!**
> Danger Signs
> Alarmingly, sudden shifts in behavior or personality could be a symptom of serious problems. A Scout may be being bullied, or may have been subjected to more serious negative influences. If this happens, it is our responsibility to find the underlying cause of the issue.

Nearly every Scout I have known thought about quitting at one time or another (including my own son). Most of their parents did what we did and compelled them to stay in Scouts until things smoothed out, (something my son appreciated later on). You may find they'll agree to set a period of time or other goal (six months, six camping trips, twelve Scout meetings) before they reach a final decision. During that time, keep your ears open and ask questions

4

The Scouter as Guide

One minute a Scouter may be a coach, the next an instructor, a little later a counselor, manager, leader, or trainer. The common thread woven into all these roles is the spirit of a helpful guide.

Two Types of Guides

Imagine a bus tour of some important city. We're seated in the air-conditioned comfort of a motor coach. As we roll along the guide explains each landmark in detail so we do not miss anything. In fact, there is so much explaining there's not much time left for questions. The guide sticks to the script, we sit behind tinted windows dutifully turning our heads to the left, then to the right, and soon the tour is over.

Contrast that tour with a hike guided by a knowledgeable outdoors person. Our group takes the lead and finds the trail. Where the trail branches, the guide will tell us which way to go if we cannot figure it out on our own. The guide does not mind if we stop now and then to admire a flower or take in the view and will happily tell us what we are looking at if we ask.

Although the guide may drop a hint here and there, the guide volunteers little information. We may miss some sights along the way or pass by interesting things, but we probably will get more out of what we *discovered* on the hike than the things the tour guide *told* us about on the bus.

Like the guide, Scouters are more responsive than directive. We inspire and encourage Scouts to explore and learn at their own speed.

Guiding Scouts is a gentle push in the right direction: a suggestion rather than a command, a question asked rather than an answer given. We can better understand the special kind of leadership required to be a good guide by contrasting three different leadership styles.

Three Types of leaders

Leadership is the keynote to success— but leadership is difficult to define, and leaders are difficult to find. I have frequently stated that "any ass can be a commander, and a trained man may often make an instructor; but a leader is more like the poet— born, not manufactured."

— ***Baden-Powell**, B.P.'s Outlook*

The best leader is one that the people are barely aware of

The next best is one who is loved and praised by the people.

Next comes one who is feared.

Worst is one who is despised.

If the leader does not have enough faith in his people,

They will not have faith in him.

The best leader puts great value in words and says little

So that when his work is finished

The people all say, "We did it ourselves!"

— **Lao Tzu,** Tao Te Ching

Although Baden-Powell and Lao Tzu lived on opposite sides of the world and wrote centuries apart, they both describe three distinct leadership styles.

Defining styles does not mean we could not find some aspect all three styles in the same person. I know that I have been all three types at one time or another.

Authoritarian Leaders

These are Lao Tzu's feared leader and Baden-Powell's commander. As a young, newly minted director of a program department at our camp, I was an insufferable authoritarian leader (I see myself at that time when I read Baden-Powell's "any ass can make a commander").

I was certainly demanding, not particularly friendly, and mistook my abrasiveness for clarity of mission. In fact, I was so brash, loud, and dictatorial I wonder any of my counselors lasted through the summer. I got my comeuppance at the end of the season when one of them had the sand to write exactly what he thought in his evaluation of my job. I owe him a great debt of gratitude; it changed me for the better.

Authoritarian leaders do get things done, but a Scouter's goal is much broader than efficiently completing tasks. Scouting has well-defined expectations, but these are not enforced in an obedience-oriented, authoritarian manner. We want our Scouts to be obedient, but we do not want them to be frightened. We encourage them to ask questions and respond by helping them find answers.

Permissive Leaders

Lao Tzu's despised leader and Baden-Powell's "trained man."

When I was hired to coach a middle school soccer team I was young enough to remember authoritarian coaches and teachers I did not like. I resolved I would be the kind of coach *everyone* liked, the "cool coach." I traded the discipline and authority a coach must have for currying favor with the team. The result was a real mess. What my players needed was a coach who would give them structure and discipline, not another "friend"; they already had plenty of friends!

Permissive leaders are usually unsure of themselves and look for reassurance in the approval and friendship of their followers. For all their effort, permissive leaders earn neither respect nor friendship. More often than not, they end up with people laughing behind their backs.

Responsive Leaders

Lao Tzu's "leader the people are barely aware of," and Baden-Powell's "poet."

Responsive leadership is a barely perceptible influence that empowers people to do things for themselves. By listening more than talking, exercising good will, and having an unshakable faith in their people, responsive leaders create an atmosphere of shared accomplishment.

Rather than dictating their own wishes, they inspire others to adopt high expectations. Their example of service is a powerful motivational force. When difficulties arise, they respond with empathy and compassion.

After many fits and starts, and years of trying, I find myself practicing responsive leadership more often than not. No doubt, there's plenty of room for improvement. If I trade self-aggrandizing authority and my desire to be accepted for an honest aspiration to serve others I find I am happier, and so are my Scouts.

My ideal Scouter practices responsive leadership enabling Scouts to do things for themselves, while offering an appropriate amount of direction to assure they remain safe and get the most from Scouting.

Overview of Three Leadership Styles

Responsive	Authoritarian	Permissive
Makes others successful	Motivated by status, respect and rewards	Looking for approval and friendship
High expectations	High demands	Low expectations
Assertive, not intrusive and restrictive	Strict rules and punishment	Few demands, rules or guidelines
Expects independent, and age-appropriate behavior	Expects conformity and compliance	Low expectations of maturity and self-control
Encourages independent reason-based decision making	Little opportunity for autonomy or decision making	Sometimes over-indulgent response to wishes or needs
Democratic	Despotic	Lenient
Explains motives clearly	Requests for explanation considered disrespectful	Tries to adapt expectations to behavior
Discussions encouraged	Orders obeyed without explanation	Allows impulsive misconduct
Responses to misbehavior are measured and consistent	Responds to misbehavior with punishment	Demands little accountability

5
Techniques for Guiding Scouts

Scouters apply the patrol system, reflection, guided discovery, inspiration, mentoring, and advancement to guide Scouts of any age. These techniques are the Scouters "virtual Swiss army knife."

Practical Application of the Patrol System

The Patrol is the unit of Scouting always, whether for work or for play, for discipline or for duty.

— ***Baden-Powell,*** Aids to Scoutmastership

We have already determined the Patrol System is the *"one essential feature"* of Scouting. Why do we have patrols? Is it just an efficient system to manage larger groups of Scouts or is it something more? We have patrols because Scouts working together in patrols are essential to achieving the aims of Scouting; there is simply no Scouting without the patrol system.

In order to get the benefits of the patrol system we apply practical measures tailored to the age of our Scouts:

Forming Patrols

Scouters have fallen into the habit of assigning Scouts to patrols based on what best serves our concerns, often to the exclusion of what Scouts want.

One of the most important reasons children become Scouts is the promise of spending time with their friends. Baden-Powell observed that children instinctually form their own "gangs." He understood the strength of those freely chosen associations and, instead of battling with this instinct, channeled it into the patrol system.

BE PREPARED!

It is not so simple...

In *The Patrol Leaders' Handbook*, Camp Chief of Gilwell and prolific writer John Thurman, had this to say about the patrol system :

"I've always been glad it isn't too easy. If all we had to do was to write 'Patrol System' over the entrance to every Troop Headquarters and a sort of miracle resulted, it would really be too simple to bother with, but fortunately, and I mean fortunately, it is not as easy as that. It does not get any easier as the years go by, and perhaps in that lies its secret, its charm and its possibilities. It always needs and always need two special qualities – the one common sense, the other effort."

We progress toward the main aim when Scouts experience the alchemy of working together to meet challenges and solve problems. Scouts make choices and resolve any difficulties those choices create. If adults make all the decisions, Scouts are managed like so many widgets instead of being individuals with the power to choose.

Allowing Scouts to choose their own patrol may look inefficient and messy; you may wonder if it is a mistake! With some practice and patience you'll see those patrols are full of happy, advancing Scouts having the time of their lives.

The Patrol is a Democracy

Scouts democratically select their youth leaders. Younger Scouts may need more adult guidance than older Scouts, but all Scouts should have some element of democratic choice.

Youth leaders in the older sections also represent their patrol to a panel or council of patrol leaders. Our work with the youth leadership of patrols and the patrol council is discussed in the chapter on Youth Engagement.

Size and Permanence of Patrols

Baden-Powell advised a patrol should number six to eight Scouts, and his advice is still sound. Fewer and the effect of working together is absent. Much larger and the interest of the individual is lost.

Ideally, the small group stays together for as long as possible. Patrols should be established, constant, groups; not formed provisionally from whatever large group of Scouts shows up for an activity. Growing familiarity with the patrol strengthens the work of interdependence and individual development.

Autonomy of Patrols

The object of the patrol method is not so much saving the Scoutmaster trouble as to give responsibility to the boy.

— Baden-Powell

A patrol should have enough independence to pursue the interest of its member Scouts. Most decisions are made and activities conducted at the level of the patrol.

Preserve the Patrol experience when large groups of Scouts participate in the same activity. Patrols always stick together, participate together, camp, hike, and work together.

Interaction Between Patrols

Patrols should be interacting with each other as often as possible. Games, competitions, challenges, and joint projects are practical ways for the developmental dynamics within patrols and within the group of patrols to do their work.

Reflection

Reflection is simply formal or informal conversation with a single Scout or a group. Reflection takes many forms; it may be scheduled or spontaneous. It can focus on one subject or encompass many. It may have a planned agenda or be off the cuff. During these conversations we stop, look where we have been and set a reference point for moving ahead, much like we do to find our way on the Appalachian Trail.

Backpacking is one of my Scouts favorite activities and the A.T. is our favorite destination. Rectangles of white paint on trees and rocks mark all 2000-plus miles of the A.T. from Maine to Georgia. In our state, Pennsylvania, the trail can be difficult to follow where it passes over stretches of rocky ground. We sometimes have to stop, turn around, and look for blazes we passed as a reference point to spot the next one.

A few minutes of intentional reflection around the campfire or sitting in a circle in the meeting room ought to be a regular habit. The length of a reflection depends on the age of the Scouts, the setting, and the subject; but five or ten minutes are usually sufficient. Sometimes I'll begin a group reflection by relating a thought or observation, but asking questions is usually the best way to get the conversation moving.

Scouts are generally eager talkers. A few ground rules for group reflection may be in order so they don't talk over one another. With groups, I find it's useful to have a leader, take turns, and keep the discussion focused; "That's a worthy subject for discussion, but just now we are talking about 'X'. Do you have thoughts on that?"

Jokers (every group has at least one!) are encouraged to participate sincerely with kindness: "Do you really feel that way or are you just kidding us? I appreciate your cheerfulness but I am more interested in what you really think."

Guided Discovery

> *Why don't I just give you a lecture? Because through my questions you learn to teach yourselves ...*
>
> *At times, you may feel that you have found the correct answer. I assure you that this is a total delusion on your part; you will never find the correct absolute and final answer. In my classroom, there is always another question that follows your answer.*
>
> — **Professor Kingsfield,** *from the 1973 film "The Paper Chase"*

We teach Scouts the crucial skill of *learning how to learn* by appealing to their natural inquisitiveness and inspiring them to work things out for themselves. Guided discovery is not making statements or lecturing, but asking questions that encourage activity.

If we lecture Scouts, we echo what they have done in school a thousand times and they react accordingly. Their attentiveness will be brief, they will show little appreciation for what's being said, and retain little of the knowledge being offered. Scouting promises engaging activity, not sitting and listening. Who could blame Scouts who find themselves in yet another classroom for feeling as if they had been cheated out of something?

Guided discovery transforms the role of the Scout from passive listener to active participant. One question follows another like a path of breadcrumbs until the Scouts discover what they need to know and do.

When Scouts discover things this way the light comes on; it is almost a physical phenomenon! They brighten up! More than just learning the right answers, they have learned to teach themselves.

Suppose we want Scouts to learn how to safely handle and maintain a pocketknife. Everything we need is laid out on a table. We could have Scouts listen as we explain, or engage them in a process of discovery:

What are the things on this table?

How are they used?

Where can you find out how they are used?

Why is it important we learn to use these tools correctly?

One question leads the next; Scouts are actively involved in supplying the answers rather than simply recording information.

Scouts learn more with their hands than with their ears, so we make sure they can start working with their hands right away. We move away from the table in a very few minutes as the Scouts start practicing and trying out the things *they* have discovered. They coach each other in those skills, and ask us questions; they are active, engaged, and happy.

Guided discovery is not limited to instruction; we employ it to counsel, train, and mentor our Scouts. *What do you think? How would you handle this? What should we do next?* Once you get the hang of guiding rather than preaching, teaching, or lecturing, you'll find it is one of the most useful tools in your kit.

Inspiration

If I communicate the love of the sea to my people,

Soon they will begin to work according to their talents;

One will weave the fabrics,

Another will cut the tree in the forest,

Another still will forge nails

Someone will observe the stars to learn how to navigate,

All will work as one.

To create the ship is not just to weave the fabrics, nor just to forge the nails, nor only to read the stars, but to long for the endless immensity of the sea.

— **Antoine de Saint-Exupéry**
A free translation of his poem Dessine-moi un bateau

One way to build a boat is the logical assignment of tasks. The result is an empty vessel with no mission, or inspiration.

If, instead, we create a vision of the sea, and inspire longing for exploration, we ignite the desire to build. There may many false starts and mistakes along the way. Nevertheless, the result is worth the effort: a vessel full of aspirations, hopes, and dreams.

Scouting is a quest, a journey, and a process of individual discovery that cannot be reduced to a set of tasks. The Scouting spirit inspires our Scouts to long for the next discovery, the next moment of enlightenment, to explore the endless immensity of their own potential.

Mentoring

> ... the business of the Scouter (and a very interesting one it is) is to draw out each boy and find out what is in him, and then to catch hold of the good and develop it to the exclusion of the bad. There is five per cent of good even in the worst character. The sport is to find it, and then to develop it on to an 80 or 90 per cent basis.
>
> — **Baden-Powel,** Aids to Scoutmastership

When Odysseus left for the Trojan War he charged Mentor with the care of his son. Mentor's name has become identified with those who share practical advice, wisdom, and knowledge with their less-experienced colleagues.

Mentors encourage sparks of interest into a fire of concentration. They help people believe they can achieve the improbable or impossible. Mentors concentrate on the talents and possibilities. They push us past perceived limitations and self-doubt to realize our full potential.

Mentors have great faith, they believe in us when others may not. They encourage action, they are there when we falter: not to pick us up, but to show us how to pick ourselves up and keep on going.

Mentoring is, as Baden-Powell said, a "sport" and an "interesting business." Mentors are not busybodies or micro-managers; they don't suffocate their subjects. Mentors are not glorified cheerleaders; they maintain objectivity and an honest interest in your welfare.

Positive Rites of Passage

Carrying backpacks for the first time, Scouts leave the familiar comforts of home and strike out on the trail. Following flashlight beams through unknown territory, they arrive at the campsite with their friends. Tents are set up, a fire is lit, and they gather around trying to shake off the cold.

They talk excitedly about tomorrow's climb over a mountain peak to the destination on the other side. They strain their imaginations in anticipation; careful to mask the uncertainty and vulnerability they feel in the volume and bravado of the conversation. Excited anticipation and the fear of the unknown make it hard to sleep that night.

In the morning, the Scouts are up and on the trail. The day unfolds in struggles and challenges that strain both backs and minds. By late afternoon, they reach the campsite on the other side of the mountain. Tired, relieved to drop their packs, they are aglow with a sense of accomplishment. They made it through! They overcame their doubts and fears, they encouraged and helped one another along the way; and now they have arrived.

Our backpacking Scouts have been through a "rite of passage," a term that bears explaining. A rite of passage has three stages:

Separation – Leaving the familiar comforts of home for a new challenge.

Transition – Enduring a period of uncertainty and vulnerability.

Accomplishment – Reaching the goal.

Understanding these stages helps us guide young people on a journey through experiences and challenges that lead to adulthood. These experiences may be familiar to us, but our Scouts are meeting these physical, mental, and spiritual challenges for the first time. They have voluntarily separated themselves from the familiar and entered into a transitional state subject to their own fears and uncertainties.

Young people want to belong to something larger than themselves, to gain acceptance, to be identified as a full member of their group. This desire is so strong, so instinctual, that it sometimes blurs the lines between good and bad. Young people are desperate to fill this void whether the group coerces them to negative, destructive behavior like a street gang, or positive, constructive activities like Scouting,

We are all familiar with the movie stereotypes of a demanding, harsh, insulting, military officer who berates and rides his recruits; the boss who ruthlessly drives his workers; or the coach who swears and yells at his players. Most of us have been subject to this sort of treatment at one time or another.

How we experienced rites of passage ourselves shapes the expectations we bring to our work as Scouters. Our instinctive reactions may be positive or negative. We may have received support and affirmation; or met with discouragement and harshness. As Scouters, we check our negative instincts and champion positive, affirming, encouraging rites of passage; we never stoop to hazing, harshness, and discouragement.

Scouting's positive rites of passage are rigorous and demanding in themselves. Harsh, critical, attitudes masquerading as rigorous determination, are corrosive and destructive—a poor way to achieve much of anything.

Some rites of passage end in clear outward symbolism, such as the ceremonial presentation of a badge. Some are more subtle transitions we mark with words of affirmation in recognition of a Scout's progress. We are never harsh or disapproving, but unfailingly supportive and understanding. Even when the going is tough, or our Scouts efforts look less than encouraging, we maintain a positive outlook. Scouters trade discouragement for honest praise. We trade demeaning, abusive hazing or "initiations" for ceremonies that honor accomplishment.

How we express honest encouragement is vitally important; we don't dispense simple platitudes or disingenuous praise. To be honestly encouraging we strive to understand the scale of the challenge from each individual Scout's perspective. Bold, outgoing, and enthusiastic, or shy, meek and fearful, we never belittle or demean a Scout's effort, even in jest. What we intend as good-natured chiding may be received as a devastating blow. We put the best face on every step forward and support each Scout's effort toward the goal.

6
Learning by Challenge & Achievement

Why? —in a world of matches? Ernest Thompson Seton answered well when a group of practical business men questioned his zest for the rubbing stick fire — said he, pointing to the ground, "You are thinking of the fire that is lighted down there," and pointing to his breast continued, "I am thinking of the fire that is kindled in here!"

Impractical it is only to staid, prosaic oldsters who have forgotten that enchanted world of dreams called childhood!

Struggling for weeks and months, a year before the days when commercial fire-by-friction sets came wrapped up in packages, experimenting and failing with countless woods and tinders, filling my room with a perpetual incense of wood smoke that in itself was reward. I still recall that fervent, youthful day when tiny coal turned to flame! —and happily the flame it kindled has never died! Must you say it is impractical?

— **Bernard Sterling Mason,** Woodcraft

There is a big difference between learning a Scouting skill and the objective: the ulterior motive, of the experience.

If the aim was to light a fire why wouldn't you just use matches? In fact, why bother with a fire when we have a perfectly good propane stove? We ask, as the "practical business men" did, aren't there more efficient ways to light a fire?

Seton had an ulterior motive: lighting a fire in hearts and minds, not just on the ground. That fire is the spirit of discovery, thirst for challenge, and love of learning. Scouting employs a progressive system of challenges based on education from within, not instruction from without.

As they advance, Scouts form positive attitudes, character, self-control, self-esteem, and usefulness. Achievements are recognized with a badge, but badges and patches are simply reference points, indicators that Scouts have attained these aims. Scouts are encouraged to progress through each stage at their own pace.

Scouts want to do exciting and engaging things, not just repetitive activities aimed at getting the next badge. Scouters are guides in this system of play and challenge. We are not academic educators working our way through a curriculum or delivering lectures and grading tests.

Scouts follow four steps to achievement: learning by doing, evaluation, reflection, and recognition. What follows is the "why" of these steps; your Scout organization has resources explaining specific systems of achievements and their administration.

Step One — Learning by Doing

Think of the learning opportunities afforded Scouts by participating in a camping trip with their patrol. They learn how to prepare themselves individually. Scouts plan, strategize, and cooperate to prepare the group. They learn by doing when they are setting up camp, cooking, exploring, and living in the natural world.

Opportunities for learning arise naturally by simply doing the things Scouts do when we apply all of the interdependent methods discussed. They progress through active, first-hand experience, not passive instruction.

We motivate our Scouts to learn things for themselves. Most of the time all we really have to do is create the opportunity and get out of the way. It is very natural to think we should explain every detail of an activity, but active exploration is our aim.

A wise Scouter learns to measure out instruction and advice in very small doses and provide every opportunity for learning by doing (see Guided Discovery earlier in this chapter).

Step Two — Evaluation

Once Scouts have learned by doing, we evaluate what they have learned with common sense, discretion, and fairness focused on the main aim. We want to avoid the extremes of being so lenient only minimal effort is required, or being so demanding only the highest standard will do.

The two basic types of evaluation are:

1. Objective Evaluation

Evaluation is a simple matter where the objective is a simple metric: such as attending a camping trip or swimming a given number of yards. Even so, we always consider individual effort.

2. Subjective Evaluation

Some less well-defined achievements require us to consider a number of factors on an individual basis.

Nearly every parent has a treasured drawing or lopsided clay statue, his or her child created. It has little objective value as a work of art. Although critics will never write about it, and it won't be displayed in a national museum the parent would never part with it! Anything that their child creates occupies a place of pride; subjectively it is priceless.

We evaluate Scouts subjectively by considering their individual abilities, challenges, and the effort they have extended. Comparing their performance to an objective ideal is like comparing that bit of artwork our child gave us up to the Mona Lisa.

Imagine achieving a subjective requirement was a literal footrace and the finish line is an ideal standard. Not all Scouts begin the race at the starting line; they begin at different places. Different home lives, characters, and habits place them ahead of or behind their fellow Scouts.

Our "average" Scout with no outstanding advantages or deficits begins the race at the starting line. Scouts with greater advantages and skills in a given area begin 75 yards ahead of the starting line. Scouts with little or no advantage or skill begin 50 yards behind the starting line.

The starter's pistol sounds, the Scouts are off and running. Gifted Scouts cover the short distance to the finish line quickly. An average Scout covers 75% of the course, another covers 25%. The Scout who began the race well behind the starting line just reaches the starting line before the race is over.

How much ground did each Scout cover?

The Scout who began farthest behind and only reached the starting line has progressed farther than the gifted Scout who reached the finish line. Our aim remains the ideal at the finish, but we evaluate progress.

This aspect of Scouting is difficult for a lot of us. It is very right, in theory, to require everyone reach the same finish line, but that's not what we are after; we want all of our Scouts to progress. This is why subjective requirements don't have a set objective standard—they are based on individual progress.

Not everyone thinks I have this right; they think we should set rigorous standards and only reward those Scouts who reach the ideal. I'd agree with them if all of our Scouts started at the same point, but they don't.

When called on to make a subjective evaluation we should ask Scouts to evaluate themselves using their own internal standards. The answer gives us all kinds of opportunities to strengthen how they think, how they see themselves, and how they encourage themselves to do better. When Scouts evaluate themselves against their own best efforts, rather than against the efforts of others, they learn to find inner motivation and purpose.

When we help them exercise an internal standard, we enable Scouts to weave the Scout oath and law into their lives and characters. They form a personal connection to the moral and ethical precepts of Scouting. They learn our internal motivations are more important than how others see us.

Step Three — Reflection

> *Keep before your mind in all your teaching that the whole ulterior motive of this scheme is to form character...*
>
> *— Baden-Powell*

Reflection helps Scouts further build on this internal standard and strengthen their connection to the Scout oath and law. Reflection is also an assessment of our work, of how effectively we are achieving the aims of Scouting.

Reflection may be an individual review of a Scout's overall progress or a group review inviting the broader perspective of the Scout's experience by more than one Scouter. Rather than re-evaluating the knowledge and skill they demonstrated we are reflecting on the process and experiences they have been through,.

Scouting is replete with metric measurements of success. Numbers are indicators, not answers; they aren't proof. Good numbers may indicate success but standing in a garage may indicate that you are a car.

In the end, our success has a single measure; did Scouting positively impact the life of the Scout? That's our aim—everything else is window dressing. We find the answer by asking the Scout.

The Scout Oath and Law define the ideal character we aim to develop through the process described in this chapter. How do we know we have succeeded in developing an individual's mental and moral qualities? What evidence do we look for?

They realize their physical, mental, and spiritual well-being not only benefits themselves, but also keeps them prepared for service.

They are able to resolve conflicts, solve problems, empathize with others, persevere through difficulties, control impulses, communicate clearly, and make thoughtful decisions.

We have succeeded when Scouts begin to see beyond their own welfare to the interests of others. They apply teamwork, engagement, commitment, to work cooperatively with others.

Step Four — Recognition

Some hiking trails above the tree line, in the tundra, or on the moors are marked with piles of stones called cairns. Hikers sometimes place a stone in the cairn to memorialize having reached the summit.

We mark progress on our journey by presenting the Scouts a symbol of their advancement (typically a badge) at a ceremony in front of their fellow Scouts and family. Like high-country cairns, these moments enshrine achievement of a goal and leave a marker for others to follow.

A few words of celebration and encouragement and time set aside for reflection on the accomplishment, bring a sense of meaning and connection to a Scout's journey. Whatever form it may take, ceremonial presentation is important and is not to be taken lightly. It is our opportunity to connect what Scouts have achieved practically (the "fire on the ground") with the growth they have experienced ("the fire in the heart").

7
Youth Engagement

Scouting is, first and foremost, for the Scouts; something they do for themselves rather than a program of activities presented for them. Scouts should be engaged in leading one another, in making decisions affecting what they do and how it is done.

In the chapter "The Scouter as a Guide," we defined our ideal responsive leadership role as a barely perceptible influence empowering young people to do things for themselves. We accomplish this in a progressive partnership: adult and youth roles are collaborative, not hierarchical.

This partnership is one of the unique facets of Scouting that adults often misunderstand. We may be reluctant to cede authority to young people, or doubt their ability to exercise authority responsibly; but youth engagement does not mean purposeless anarchy. Scouting has boundaries in the same way lines chalked on a playing field describe the boundaries of a game. Both Scouts and Scouters observe these boundaries in a reciprocal commitment based on mutual trust and patience.

I've outlined the basics of these progressive roles:

Adult and Youth Roles in Youth Engagement

Age	Adult leadership role	Scout leadership role
Childhood 5–9 years	Leading and instructing Sharing skills and ideas. Modeling responsible leadership.	Helping in simpler tasks and decision-making. Simple peer-to-peer sharing.
Pre-Teen 9–13 years	Turning over the reins. Responding to growing capability for responsible self-determination. Encouraging more discovery and peer-to-peer instruction.	Directed leadership roles with intermediate tasks. More influence in choosing activities and decision-making. Intermediate peer-to-peer instruction.
Teens 13–16 years	Mentoring, observing Responding to the Scout's initiatives and interests. Less direction, more advising.	More independent to fully independent leadership roles. Great influence on choosing activities and decision-making. Peer-to-peer instruction.
Young Adults 16–21 years	Facilitation. Almost exclusively providing resources and administrative support.	Independent leadership roles. Responsible for choosing activities and decision-making.

A Simple Formula

"Train em' trust em' and let them lead"

— **William Hillcourt,** *Scoutmaster's Handbook*

"Green Bar" Bill Hillcourt, author of many Scouting handbooks, had a simple formula for engaging youth in leadership:

Train Them

We wouldn't begin instructing Scouts learning to tie a square knot with a long theoretical discourse on knotting; we put ropes in their hands and let them try.

The most effective way to develop as a leader is by leading. Training leaders means engaging them actual leadership. Some preparation is important, but leadership skill develops as you lead, not in a training session. Elaborate training schemes are long on instruction and short on experience. Many Scouters tend to over-explain and over-instruct in a way Scouts find frustrating.

Don't overload new youth leaders with theoretical information, give them the basics, and let them at it. Follow up with reflection and mentoring to steer developing leaders toward confidence and success.

Trust Them

Parents who teach their children to drive are uncomfortable at best and even a little panicked from time to time! Letting Scouts engage in leadership feels a lot like sitting in the passenger seat while a student driver steers the car.

We may understand how important it is to let go, but letting go is never easy. Trusting youth leaders is always a challenge; but it gets easier as you see what they are capable of achieving.

Let Them Lead

Do not give a Scout responsibility and undermine it with continual interference. As aloof and disaffected as they may appear Scouts are seeking your approval. They need an avuncular, friendly, understanding coach, not a doting busybody.

Their shortcomings may be many, their failures and oversights may outnumber successes, but if they are encouraged toward honest effort and imbued with confidence, they rise to the challenge.

Real Responsibility

There is no *real* responsibility if we eliminate the possibility of failing. Naturally, we want our Scouts to succeed, but this does not mean we absolutely protect them from failing. We ought to expect, and learn to welcome, bumps and setbacks along the way; they are a vital part of our developmental journey.

A championship team usually suffers a loss somewhere along the road to victory. The difference between a championship season and a losing record hinges on learning the lessons failure teaches. Handled the right way, bumps and setbacks can be a source of intense motivation.

More than one athlete has shed tears of frustration over a bad play. When there is a fumble during a football game recovering the ball becomes a team challenge. If a player fumbles the ball, teammates respond with a pat on the back and encouragement to get back in the game. Scouters respond to mistakes and failures with the same good humor, encouragement, and commiseration. We see failures as inevitable, yet valuable, opportunities to grow, not as crimes to prosecute and punish.

Scouts are sensitive to failure and how it affects their standing in the eyes of their peers. Praise publically and correct in private, never subjecting Scouts to humiliation or embarrassment. If our reaction to difficulties is finding fault or being harsh, few Scouts will be willing to take on responsibility. We can encourage accountability without dramatics, punishment, or bad feelings.

Inspiring Initiative

Expect a great deal of your Patrol Leaders and nine times out of ten they will play up to your expectation; but if you are going always to nurse them and not to trust them to do things well, you will never get them to do anything on their own initiative.

— **Baden-Powell,** B.P.'s Outlook

Many Scouters tried (once or twice) to engage Scouts in meaningful leadership. When the Scouts did not respond as they hoped, they grew impatient, and became discouraged all too quickly. Disappointed Scouters tend to reserve important decisions and authority to themselves.

This cycle repeats itself; Scouts get one or two tries, do not respond as expected, and Scouters stop trying. If I challenge Scouters on this, they tell me "our Scouts just do not do what they are supposed to do, they have no initiative." Their Scouts may have leadership titles, but without any real responsibility or authority.

Anyone lacking authority waits for those in authority to initiate action. Scouts with no authority have no initiative. They'll wait until Scouters do things for them. We ought to expect Scouts developing leadership skills take more time to get things done, make mistakes, and forget things. What seems routine to us may be totally new to a Scout. It is unfair to expect an inexperienced Scout to respond the same way an experienced adult would.

Youth engagement is not a switch we throw: it is seed we plant. We grow impatient if a light switch does not instantly make the light come on. If a seed does not sprout the minute it is planted, we are not surprised — we know this sort of thing takes time.

Scouters plant seeds, water the garden, pull the weeds, look for sprouts, and nurture new plants. When we engage youth in leadership, we nurture initiative, keep it free from interference, and watch it grow.

Scouts show initiative if we learn to look for it. New leaders are vulnerable; they need reassurance to get past the first few problems. Instead of focusing on what is wrong with a Scout's performance, look for the least sign of initiative and support it, no matter how small. Maintain an environment that helps grow initiative and leadership, and you'll reap great rewards for your Scouts.

Observing from a Distance

Understanding what happens when we observe Scouts and how our presence alters what they do is a key part of engaging youth in leadership. Two effects from the science of physics help explain this. The observer effect states "observation changes the object being observed." For example, a tire pressure gauge releases air from the tire, thus changing the pressure as we observe it. The proximity effect occurs when two atoms come into proximity and the electrons on the two atoms reorganize.

Scouts react when we are in the proximity. They tend to see any nearby adult as the default leader. Just standing nearby can reorganize the dynamic between youth leaders and Scouts. If an adult is too close by, or offers too much advice, Scouts do not have a fighting chance of engaging in leadership.

If we sit at the table during a youth leader's meeting, they do not have much chance of talking and debating openly. If we stand by watching as Scouts lead an activity, they have one eye on us and one eye on what they are doing. When we stride into a patrol campsite, activity stops and the attention turns to us.

Ideally, we observe from a respectful distance so we do not affect the behavior we are observing. Think about the way ornithologist studies birds: quietly, at a distance, shielded from view.

I am not saying Scouts should always be on their own regardless of the activity or the level of their behavior. We account for age, the nature of the activity, ability, and temperament of the Scouts in question. If safety or propriety becomes an issue we step in. Short of that, we keep our distance and allow Scouts the latitude to lead without interference.

Be Resilient

Youth engagement in its earliest stages may look like things are moving backwards. Chaos and inconsistency are challenging if we have high expectations for order and consistency. To get past this stage, Scouters must have an exceptional capacity for adversity and uncertainty.

We know Scouts do not perform at the same level as adults. We must be quick to encourage and slow to interfere; always keep in mind they are developing leaders, not seasoned professionals.

Finding the Advisor's Voice

There's a subtle, yet important, difference in directing youth leaders to do things and motivating them to get things done. Scouters have to find the "advisor's voice."

I don't mean tone or volume, but the motivation behind what you say. The advisor's voice is really the voice of the Scouts. An advisor articulates the concerns of the Scouts to motivate youth leaders to service.

Why do youth leaders do the things they do? Is it to satisfy demands made by the Scouter? No. Youth leaders aren't serving adults, they are serving their fellow Scouts.

What do Scouts need from their youth leaders? They want to go camping, advance, and do Scouting with their friends! Because Scouts don't always articulate these needs clearly, they need someone to speak for them.

When we use the advisors voice, our youth leaders are hearing the voice of the Scouts they serve. What they do isn't for our benefit or to save us the work of doing it ourselves, but to make Scouting come alive for their Scouts.

If Scouters take a directive role, youth leadership is answerable to the Scouter. If Scouters take an advisory role, youth leaders are answerable to the Scouts they serve.

Value the Discovery Process.

After much trial and error, Thomas Edison discovered tungsten steel made a durable light bulb filament. Scouts similarly try many ways to solve problems or get things done. We ought to support this trial and error even when we suspect the approach may fail—although we guard against trial and error that becomes inappropriate or dangerous.

The important distinction between Edison and our Scouts is Edison was looking for an unknown and our youth leaders are looking for answers we probably know already. If we supply answers we deny Scouts the more powerful, lasting experience of discovering answers for themselves.

Coordinating with other Scouters in advisory roles preserves this atmosphere of discovery. Only one advisor ought to direct a youth leader when needed. If other Scouters have concerns, they go to the Scouter advising the youth leader, not the youth leader directly. I have seen a group of Scouters "being helpful" run youth leaders ragged!

Five minutes of experience beats five hours of instruction. Trial and error shows youth leaders what they could not otherwise know or understand.

Citizenship and Leadership

A good leader and a good citizen both have a sense of individual responsibility and the desire to be of service to others. In many ways, leadership and citizenship are synonymous. When we engage youth in leadership, we are engaging them in learning the skills of citizenship.

We are not all destined to become leaders in the classic sense, by directing others or heading up a group. There is much more to leadership than simply being in command. Leadership consists of four basic components:

Four Leadership Components

Be Prepared – Self-Leadership.

Before they lead others Scouts must care for their own spiritual, mental, and physical needs. If Scouts do not care for themselves, they limit their ability to help others.

Do Your Best – Leading by Following

Following cooperatively requires a positive attitude and positive actions that contribute to the activity.

Lend a Hand – Assisting Leadership

We assist our fellow Scouts by being kind, friendly, and helpful at every opportunity.

Lead the Way – Directive Leadership

Scouts who lead themselves, follow cooperatively and help their fellow Scouts are prepared to become directive leaders. We look for evidence of these four components in our Scouts as they progress through their journey:

Milestones for Younger Scouts

Self-Leadership

A growing ability to look beyond themselves to how their actions and attitudes affect others. We help them associate good actions and attitudes and the Scout Oath and Law.

Leading by Following

Growing a basic sense of altruism and desire to serving others. They find satisfaction in helping others before fulfilling our own desires.

Assisting Leadership

Scouts help with simple tasks and work cooperatively together.

Directive Leadership

Younger Scouts take on direct roles in games ceremonies and activities with appropriate oversight.

Milestones for Older Scouts

Self-Leadership

A strong sense of how their actions and speech affects others. They associate the Scout Oath and Law with their actions and attitudes.

Cooperative Leadership

Readily help others with little or no prompting; have a heightened sense of fairness and empathy. Growing more tolerant and accepting of differing points of view and levels of ability.

Assisting Leadership

Ideals of service and cooperation are strong. Pride in group accomplishments over individual achievements; they associate their well-being with that of the group.

Directive Leadership

Self-directed and self-supervised much of the time. Observant adults reinforce boundaries that inform good decisions.

Milestones for Senior Scouts

Self-Leadership

Moral and ethical obligations of the Scout Oath and Law have a central place in the life of the Scout.

Cooperative Leadership

Welcoming, supportive and helpful toward their fellow Scouts. Confident in their outlook and relationships.

Assisting Leadership

Fully formed ideals of service and readily subordinate their needs to those of others. A real desire to offer help and to make a difference.

Directive Leadership

Keen sense of responsibility to lead fairly and well, with little to no oversight. Readily seek advice and assistance to help them stay on the right track.

8
Outdoor Adventure

For those who have eyes to see and ears to hear, the forest is at once a laboratory, a club, and a temple.

— *Baden-Powell*

Baden-Powell chose the word "Scouting" to invoke "the work and attributes of backwoodsmen, explorers, hunters, seamen, airmen, pioneers and frontiersmen." Adventure in the great outdoors is elemental to our success; Scouts strive to find our place in and form a living connection with the natural environment.

Human civilization developed in the natural world. The ideals of community, interdependence, and personal responsibility were elemental to our ancestor's survival in an often-hostile environment. Scouts rebuild civilization each time they gather wood, build a fire, cook food, and shelter themselves from the elements. They gain first-hand knowledge of life's necessities in meeting the physical, mental, and social challenges of outdoor life.

Nature's richness and complexity lends itself to introspection and fellowship away from the artifices of society that alienate us from one another. If we do not connect to the natural world, we lose our connection to each other.

There's a vast difference between being housed in a tent and going camping. Big gatherings and pre-planned events have their place, but Scouts should be planning and leading their adventures rather than just participating in ones prepared for them.

I think sometimes we miss the point because we imagine Scouts want entertainment. Scouting's real work is not accomplished in elaborate activities designed to amuse, but in the simple day-to-day concerns of camp life.

The Question of Scale

Scouts should always be working in patrols not in vast herds. Again, "patrol" is any organized small group.

Whenever possible each patrol should camp as though other patrols did not exist. They should be self-contained and self-led.

Camping at the patrol scale accomplishes the real work of Scouting. Establishing the campsite, setting up tents, cooking, getting water, keeping things clean, and living in some comfort may seem inconsequential, but it isn't. These practical concerns of camp sharpen leadership skills, encourage interdependence, and require personal responsibility. We are susceptible to the fallacy that good things are even better if they are larger. Each step away from the Patrol is overlaid with an ever-burgeoning bureaucracy that obscures the real work of Scouting. In an attempt to make things "bigger and better," we are in danger of losing focus on the target—the individual Scouts and their Patrol.

Outfitting

The temptation is to buy this or that bit of indispensable camp kit has been too strong and we have gone to the blessed woods handicapped with a load fit for a pack mule. That is not how to do it. Go light, and the lighter the better so that you have the simplest material for health comfort and enjoyment.

— **Nessmuk**, Camping and Woodcraft

George W. Sears (Nessmuk) penned this in 1906; a century later, the temptation to overload ourselves with gadgets is even greater. What we carry into the woods should pass Nessmuk's simple test of health, comfort, and enjoyment. The joy of camping hinges not on how much we bring, but on how little. When we are outfitting and preparing our Scouts and ourselves, we should keep in mind that we are seeking a closer connection to the natural world, not to totally insulate ourselves from it.

The Question of Risk

I was helping lead a high school group on an ambitious backpacking trip in New York's Adirondack high peaks region. Our trip began in the rain on a November night after a long drive. A creek crossing the next morning set us back an hour or two because the creek was swollen by the previous day's rainfall. We were late starting our climb over a high pass that afternoon, and daylight was running out.

With no place to bivouac in that terrain, we had little choice but to keep moving. We hiked through the night and arrived at our destination just before daybreak the next morning. We had skirted disaster, but needlessly put our group in serious danger.

As a teenager, I was part of a high school group that travelled to Western Canada and Alaska. The adults who led us were well-intentioned, but had little experience or skill when it came to wilderness travel. In attempting to scale a mountain in the Alaskan panhandle one of our group lost his footing and fell to his death.

These two cautionary tales illustrate a simple point — anyone entrusted with the care of children cannot be complacent about the risk inherent in wilderness adventure. Any experienced wilderness traveler will tell you that outdoor accidents are caused by inexperience, lack of training, bravado, and/or arrogance.

I outline the basic practices that you should augment with your Scouting association's specific directions.

Conscientious, Qualified Supervision

Trained, experienced, and confident leaders should supervise activities with the necessary skills required to respond to emergencies.

Fitness of Participants

Participants should have the physical, developmental, and mental capacities to undertake the activity. They must also have the requisite skills to execute every aspect of the activity safely.

Never Alone

Any inherently risky activity should be undertaken with a group or partner who is monitoring your progress as you monitor theirs.

Safe Conditions

The area and equipment used for the activity are free of hazards, designed for the use intended, and properly maintained. Conditions are monitored and the activity only proceeds under suitable weather. Sufficient protective equipment is on hand for all participants and used properly.

Plans, Response, and Communications

Activities follow a conscientious plan developed by knowledgeable people. Leaders should be able to communicate with participants and with the emergency response system. Adequate supplies and skills are on hand to respond to injuries or emergencies.

Risk and Age

Imagine we are standing on a six-foot tall platform with a ladder to the ground. It is riskier to jump, but it is quicker and bolder than taking the ladder.

An adult takes the ladder, thinking it is safer than jumping. A teenager jumps, valuing getting down quicker and showing off. To the teenage mind, the benefits of speed and showiness outweigh the risk of jumping. Jumping seems foolish to a reasonable adult, to a teenager it makes perfect sense!

Despite what you have heard, teenagers do not think they are invulnerable. Teens take unacceptable risks because they weigh benefits more heavily than risks, not necessarily because they are willful or impulsive.

Risks are less appealing if Scouts understand the direct benefit from alternative, safer courses of action. Teens are more concerned with what others think of them than the reality of risk. Promote positive images of safe behavior and negative images of unsafe ones.

Help Scouts build the self-confidence to recognize and reject risky behavior or remove themselves from risky situations. Limit unsupervised exposure to risky situations and occupy their time with positive activities.

9
Constructive Discipline

Discipline is not gained by punishing a child for a bad habit, but by substituting a better occupation, that will absorb his attention, and gradually lead him to forget and abandon the old one.

— **Baden-Powell,** Aids to Scoutmastership

Years ago, on an archeological dig, I unearthed a shard of pottery several thousand years old. The hands that shaped that bit of clay left marks still crisp and clear centuries later. Could the artisan have imagined those impressions would last so long? Young people are impressionable. For good or ill, what we do and say leaves indelible marks.

Scouts have little real control over their lives. Their families, instincts, and experiences define their behavior; intentional misbehavior is relatively rare. It's difficult to attribute intention to someone who has not yet developed the faculties required to make cogent decisions.

There is no greater test of a Scouter's skill and goodwill than how maintain discipline and accountability. We cannot always control our Scout's actions, but we can control our reactions. Scouters rarely do objectively bad things, but they do occasionally react in ways that from an adult perspective may seem right in theory, but are simply out of place in the context of Scouting.

As children, we all knew how to *act* virtuous, attentive, and obedient even when we felt otherwise. We could act compliant in the hopes it would moderate the punishment we received or that we would just be left alone. Of course, as soon as the adults were out of sight we dropped the act and did whatever we wanted to!

On one level, we understand this familiar subterfuge is part of growing up, and of asserting one's autonomy and independence. No matter how understanding we try to be, bad behavior tries our patience.

In their experimental quest to become adults, Scouts do and say things that require correction. Scouters are not disciplinarians or mediators of punishment. We do not employ negative reinforcement or hold the fear of punishment over Scouts. We do not use forced physical activity—such as pushups—or deal in demerits, suspensions, or probations.

Scouting's positive, constructive, methods effectively prevent most bad behavior by encouraging good behavior. If difficulties arise, we apply constructive discipline. This is not to say we tolerate bad behavior. Our expectations are nothing less than those virtues defined in the Scout Oath and Law.

Appropriate Reactions to Bad Behavior

Scouters dealing with difficult behavior should first quiet their own emotional response. A bad decision is neither intended to hurt us, nor as a personal affront. If we respond emotionally, Scouts view consequences as a judgment imposed on them, rather than as the direct result of their decisions.

We make the best of difficult situations if we understand the difference between addressing behavior and judging an individual. We may be disappointed in the behavior, but we aren't disappointed in the Scout.

Compassion and kindness are strengths, not weaknesses. Angry, shaming Scouters have angry, shaming, (and scared) Scouts. Compassionate, kind Scouters have compassionate, kind, Scouts. Which Scouts do you suppose have a better record of behavior?

Applying Constructive Discipline

Our aim is the formation of an internal standard based on the Oath and Law. Constructive discipline is more about asking questions than issuing judgments. We listen carefully and help Scouts discover the moral and ethical ideals bearing on the situation.

Here is an example of what I mean. A Scouter is having a conversation with a Scout who, on a dare, collapsed a fellow Scout's tent.

Scouter: Can you tell me what happened here?

Scout: I knocked John's tent down.

Scouter: Why did you do that?

Scout: I don't know.

Scouter: Well, I have a hard time believing that you just suddenly decided to do that, what were you thinking?

Scout: Nothing.

Scouter: So nobody suggested that it would be a good idea, you came up with it on your own?

Scout: Well, the other Scouts said I should.

Scouter: Did it turn out to be a good idea?

Scout: No.

Scouter: I can think of several points of the Scout Law you must have forgotten for a moment, can you?

Scout: I don't know.

Scouter: Really? You don't know?

Scout: No.

Scouter: Perhaps you need some time to think about this. If you aren't ready to talk to me now, you can sit here and wait for a while, I can be back in 15 or 20 minutes.

Scout: Okay—what do you want me to say?

Scouter: I want you to answer my question.

Scout: I know it was wrong; it's no big deal, I won't do it again.

Scouter: Well it's a big deal to me, and it's a big deal to John. Can you see that?

Scout: Yes.

Scouter: How do you make this right?

Scout: I could apologize to John.

Scouter: Anything else?

Scout: I can set his tent back up.

Scouter: Sounds good to me. I know the last thing you want do is sit here talking to me, but I can't ignore actions like this. Please make this right with John. Before you do, tell me what part of the Scout Law you forgot.

Scout: To be trustworthy, and maybe friendly, and kind.

Scouter: See, I knew you had not forgotten that. We all forget ourselves from time to time and do things we regret; can I trust you to make this right and not do it again?

Scout: I suppose so.

Scouter: Good. I knew I could count on you, the next time we talk let's have something better to talk about.

Note that the Scouter is not issuing judgments so much as asking questions to help the Scout understand how his actions affect others, and tie that to the Oath and Law.

A helpful attitude turns a difficult situation into an opportunity to strengthen character and exercises a Scout's internal standard. When Scouts have a strong sense of personal responsibility and hold themselves accountable for their actions, we have travelled a long way toward achieving the aim of our work.

Consequences and Punishment

When Scouts behave badly, we differentiate between *proportionate consequences* and *corrective punishment*. Proportionate consequences are the direct result of misbehavior: such as sitting out an activity, being restricted from using something—such as a knife—that was misused, resolving a conflict, or cleaning up a mess. Corrective punishment is any sanction beyond proportionate consequences.

Scouters and youth leaders *should not apply corrective punishment*. Systems of corrective punishments, such as demerits, forced physical activity, or the like, are completely out of place in Scouting. A system of rules and sanctions require enforcement and policing. Scouters are neither enforcers nor police.

Misbehavior is met with constructive discipline that determines appropriate proportionate consequences. In the example I shared, the proportionate consequences were making an apology and setting up the tent.

What if a Scout keeps misbehaving? What happens if our Scout keeps knocking down other tents? What if the behavior damaged something or injured someone?

Repetitive or serious bad behavior is discussed with the Scouts and their parents. We tell the parents we've imposed proportionate consequences and it is now the parents' option to employ any corrective punishment.

If, after this initial talk with their parents, Scouts' misbehavior continues, their parents are told the Scout cannot continue to participate until they assure us this behavior will not be repeated.

Positive Reinforcement

The boy is not governed by don't, but is led by do.

— **Baden-Powell,** Aids to Scoutmastership

We probably all recall some landmark in our childhood where we failed and the adults around us reacted with anger or shame. Scouters need to learn how to be disappointed in behavior without being disappointed in the Scout. We want our Scouts to *do better*; we don't achieve this by making them *feel worse.*

Bad behavior diminishes if we make a habit of looking for and recognizing good behavior. A few words of honest praise from someone you respect are a powerful force for good.

10

Lions, Tigers & Bears

Let us not pray to be sheltered from dangers but to be fearless when facing them.

— **Rabindranath Tagore,** Fruit Gathering

Lions and tigers and bears! Oh, my!

— *Dorothy*

Truly difficult or dangerous situations in Scouting are few. General safety in the outdoors is discussed in the section on *Managing Risk* in the Outdoor Adventure chapter. Resolving most behavioral problems with Scouts is addressed in the Constructive Discipline chapter.

A few other difficult situations require discussion: problem Scouters, child abuse or neglect, bullying, and homesickness.

Problem Scouters

Every so often, adults volunteer in Scouting because they crave authority, enjoy aggrandizing themselves, or want to impose their particular idea of how the world ought to be.

Scouting programs are adaptable, but this adaptability sometimes leads to misuse. Some Scouters ignore or alter clearly expressed policies and rules. They are convinced they know better.

Some intimidate Scouts and, often, many of their fellow adults. They may be brash, harsh, and demanding. They expect respect and obedience, and few people are willing to stand up to them. Some labor under the narcissistic delusion they have extraordinary authority and knowledge.

Proper training and goodwill are important preventative measures, but sometimes you have to take a problem Scouter head on. Plain talk from a friend sometimes helps. Other times direction or action from a higher authority is required.

> **BE PREPARED!**
> Traditions and Habits
> Scouting's many hallowed traditions connect us to the past and provide a bridge into the future. There is a difference between tradition and repetitive habits divorced from their original intent.
>
> You may have heard the story of the cook who always cuts the end off a roast before putting it in the oven because mother did. Mother did this because her mother did. Grandmother tells you she cut the end off the roast because her oven was too small for a whole roast!
>
> It is all too easy to think the folks who came before us did things the right way. Scouting's traditions ought to be continuously examined and tested to be sure what we are doing is actually what we ought to be doing instead of cutting the ends off the roast

Scouters' accomplishments, past service, or their own

sense of self-importance do not outweigh the best interests of our Scouts. The simple rule is that in the battle of interests, the best interest of the Scouts always wins.

When the actions of a Scouter negatively affect the interest of Scouts, it is time to act, and to act decisively. Without speedy, decisive action, problem Scouters can cause a great deal of damage.

Child Abuse and Neglect

There are two poisonous snakes native to the area where I live: the timber rattler and the copperhead. After 40 or so years spent in the outdoors, I can count the times I have run across these snakes on one hand. I know how to identify both, how to avoid them, and what to do if they bite.

It is likely you have about the same chance of encountering incidents of abuse and neglect that I have of running across a copperhead or a timber rattler. Nevertheless, every responsible Scouter needs to know how to identify abuse or neglect and what to do if you encounter them.

We know how to summon help in a medical emergency; we would do it without thinking. We should not be afraid ask for help if we suspect a child is being abused. Protecting our children is a community responsibility. Organizational safeguards are not sufficient on their own; Scouters are the first line of defense. Recognizing and responding to abuse should be a key part of training for any volunteer working with children. Despite how distressing and uncomfortable all this may be, we must not be reluctant to take action and keep children safe.

Trust your instincts. Our responsibility is to report, not investigate. We do not need "evidence" or even actual knowledge of abuse; reasonable cause, good-faith suspicion, or belief based on observations is enough.

Nearly anyone would feel reluctant to report *suspected* abuse; the stakes are high on both sides of the question. An unsubstantiated report may cause turmoil, but a child may be unalterably harmed if we fail to report.

Any youth-oriented organization is vulnerable to exploitation. People intent on stealing money go where the money is and exploit any laws they find in the security system. People intent on abusing children are going to find places children congregate and exploit any weakness in the policies and procedures that protect them.

> **BE PREPARED!**
> Know What to Do
> Know your local laws and responsibilities that apply to reporting abuse and neglect.
> Take advantage of training and follow the practices and policies set by your Scouting organization.

In recent years, we have all seen the news unfold, as incidents of abuse, sometimes decades old, become known. We have learned that people who were supposed to protect children actually protected abusers. They were more concerned with the reputation of their institution than the safety of children. Organizational secrecy, shame, and the understandable reluctance of individuals to act on suspicions of abuse empower abusers.

What About Bullying?

Ranging from name calling to physical assault, bullying satisfies a bully's needs on a primal, instinctual level. Many bullies do not realize what they are doing; talking seems to do little, as do normal disciplinary measures. Punishment may backfire and lead to even more bullying.

Bullies express their insecurities by exploiting the insecurity of others. In some cases, they may have a serious mental or social imbalance and need professional help.

Prevention is the best measure. Foster an environment of mutual respect, acceptance, and tolerance, and bullying will never gain a foothold.

Address incidents of bullying immediately. They do not resolve themselves. If bullying is not stopped, more often than not, it gets worse.

Over-reacting to bullying tends to make things even more complicated, however. Responding with punishment or anger only adds fuel to the fire. Do not address the situation until you have calmed yourself down—ask for help if you need it.

Ask the Scouts to explain their behavior; ask if they can reconcile what they are doing with the Scout Oath and Law. Help them understand how their behavior is harming others. Have them take positive action by making amends, apologies, doing a good deed, or restoring any damaged property.

Follow up; ask them how things are going, have them explain what parts of the Oath and Law they are acting on. Encourage good behavior by taking notice of every positive action.

Scouts have many different reasons for being involved. I cannot help but think our most difficult Scouts are with us because they really need our assistance. They need opportunities for positive attention and building self-esteem, something bullies are looking for in all the wrong ways.

Curing Homesickness

Away from familiar surroundings or people, Scouts may become homesick. Homesickness is a sense of dread or helplessness that leads to depression, sadness, frustration, and even anger. Homesickness may have physical symptoms, such as indigestion, headaches, nausea, and tears. Homesickness is relatively easy to cure, but it is a very real problem that should not be ignored.

Many of the causes of homesickness can be avoided when parents and Scouts have thorough information on our destination, the length of the stay, and the expectations of the activity. Experts recommend bringing "transitional objects": a couple of mementos from home (such as photos or toys) help relieve uncomfortable feelings.

Homesickness sometimes resolves itself with a friendly talk. Keep a homesick Scout active; encourage group activities and responsibilities. Writing home may be helpful, but actually speaking to someone may be better.

College counselors and chaplains tell us some first year students experience homesickness serious enough to affect their studies. Scouts who encounter and overcome homesickness at an early age are better prepared for these experiences.

11
Bringing It All Together

Advancement is like a suntan; something you get naturally whilst having fun in the outdoors.

— *Baden-Powell*

Boys or girls learn there is a thing called "Scouting," tell their parents they want to be a Scout, and appear at the doorway of our meeting room. Just inside, there is a flurry of energetic activity; Scouts are moving in several directions at once. An older Scout sees them standing there, asks a question or two and after a quick introduction our new Scouts join in.

"We're going camping next weekend, want to go?"

"Sure!"

"Okay, how about working with the Antelope patrol, would that be okay?"

"I guess so."

The patrol leader introduces the newcomer to the patrol and the group starts working on preparing for the trip. They are talking about menus, what needs to be packed; it is all a little overwhelming and exciting!

Before the meeting closes, the new Scout meets the Scouter guiding the group. A few questions, a bit of paperwork, and the promise to have parents get in touch, and then back to the patrol. At the end of the meeting, the Scout in charge introduces the newcomer to the group, and the journey is already well underway.

More meetings follow, they are exciting and interesting. There is not a lot of sitting down or listening, no lectures, no reading assignments, and no homework; just a lot of real hands-on engagement all about getting outdoors on the next camping trip.

The Antelope patrol does everything together; they practice, plan, and play as a team. They also argue and quarrel; everything is organized one moment and dissolves into chaos the next. When needed, an older Scout or a Scouter helps them return to order, but they need this reminder less and less, as time goes by.

Soon the much-anticipated day arrives with the excited pandemonium of packing gear, getting into cars, the drive to the camping ground, a hike to the camping spot. The Antelope patrol shows our new Scout what they need to know, sets up their tents, arranges their kitchen; they are off and running!

There are some purposeful activities on the schedule, there are games and fun, quiet moments, there are meals to make, trails to hike, and stories to tell. A campfire, a sing-a-long, some skits; finally, a word from the Scouter, and a well-earned night's sleep.

Our new Scout has learned and experienced much, simply doing what Scouts do: chosen and packed gear, set up a tent, cooked a meal, tended a fire, and maybe even tied a knot or two. More importantly, the Scout has started to navigate the complex interrelationships of the patrol; the joy of cooperation, learning to follow, seeing what it is like to lead; the thousand everyday decisions needed to move along and get along.

When there is a spare moment, the patrol leader asks to look at the new Scout's handbook. It turns out many things done in the course of the camp-out are requirements toward a badge. A few questions and strokes of the pen record the progress, and it is off to the next activity.

Our new Scout has heard the Oath and Law recited, even read it in the handbook. Although it may be a while before they are committed to memory, these ideals have begun to find a place in our new Scout's heart. Months and years pass, and those ideals take root as the Scout becomes ever more capable, and takes this knowledge into adulthood.

Ask Scouts about what they did, a smile comes to their faces, their eyes light up, and they tell you about the fun they had! Ask them exactly what they learned, why it was fun, and most struggle to tell you precisely what that was.

Scouts experience Scouting as "fun" even though they cannot define exactly what "fun" is. Fun is important, fun is vital, but fun has a bad reputation. Some adults think "fun" is a waste of time or distraction from serious work, such as "doing requirements," but they are mistaken.

It is the fun, and lessons learned in the process of having fun, that actually achieves the main aim of Scouting. It is not the skills, the paperwork, and the badges. It is not sermons, or lectures from adults. Scouting is meaningful fun, a game with a purpose.

When we turn the key on the meeting room door, drive a carload of Scouts to their next adventure, or do any of the multitude of mundane administrative tasks required, we create the opportunity for our Scouts to do Scouting.

Then we step back and let them make the most of it.

12

Always Travelling; Never Arriving

A hundred years from now it will not matter what my bank account was, the sort of house I lived in, or the kind of car I drove. But the world may be different, because I was important in the life of a boy.

- Forest Witcraft, Scouting Magazine, October 1950

Scouting's values are nothing new; they have been part of every enlightened society throughout human history. They are too broad for any one religious or political point of view, or any one organization to own them.

We look on our fellow Scouts as we hope they look on us. We understand a Scout may hold different beliefs, or practice different customs, without diminishing our own. Beyond simple tolerance, we cheerfully and bravely share the world and ourselves with those we may disagree with on some things, because we share much more in common.

We understand this diversity is the whole genius of Scouting—that every pledge, Oath, Law, policy, and procedure ought to be subservient to this simple concept. My Scouting movement, your scouting movement, our Scouting movement is bigger than the things that divide us.

Perhaps the next great leap of humanity will come when we fully embrace the common good in each other. Scouting will have a part in this as Baden-Powell expressed in his last message to Scouters:

> *Our aim is to produce healthy, happy, helpful citizens; to eradicate the prevailing narrow self-interest; personal, political, sectarian and national, and to substitute for it a broader spirit of self-sacrifice and service in the cause of humanity; and thus to develop mutual goodwill and cooperation not only within our own country but abroad, between all countries.*
>
> *Experience shows that this consummation is no idle or fantastic dream, but is a practical possibility — if we work for it... Therefore you are not only doing a great work for your neighbor's children, but are also helping in practical fashion to bring to pass God's Kingdom of peace and goodwill upon earth. So, from my heart, I wish you Godspeed in your effort.*

I've hung in there long enough to see some of my Scouts grow up and journey far into adulthood. Scouts from my first years as a Scouter are approaching 40 years of age (!); it seems an impossibly short time has passed since we were camping together.

My wife and I receive wedding invitations, birth announcements, and welcome visits from old Scouts. We are deeply appreciative and touched to be a continuing part of their lives.

We were invited to the wedding of one of the men she calls "our boys" and I was asked to a reader. We sat with "our boys" in the church and they stifled a laugh when I managed to brush the microphone rather loudly with the paper I read from.

At the reception, we almost all fit around one table. I listened to all of the news and thought back to when they were just teenagers at camp. I was so pleased to hear of their work and their lives and to see them happy. Teachers, writers, engineers, businessmen, and public servants; they've chosen wonderful partners and many of them have children of their own.

Although we see each other infrequently, the easygoing bond of fellowship remains strong. I can only hope each of us is blessed to know such good people who carry forward the good things that they gained as Scouts.

I am still out camping with my young Scouts watching them pass through familiar experiences; the first camping trip, the first week away from home, the year they seemed to grow an inch every month, watching as they discover greater confidence and skill.

It's been a wonderful journey, and so much more lies ahead!

References

Baden-Powell, Robert. **Aids to Scoutmastership**. New York and London: G. P. Putnam's Sons, 1920.

Baden-Powell, Robert. **Scouting and Youth Movements**. London: Ernst Benn, Ltd., 1929.

Bstan-'dzin-rgya-mtsho, Dalai Lama XIV; Howard C. Cutler. **The Art of Happiness: A Handbook for Living**. New York: Riverhead Books, 1998.

Davies, William Henry. **The Collected Poems**. London: A. C. Fifield, 1916.

Hillcourt, William. **Scoutmaster's Handbook,** Fourth Edition. New York: Boy Scouts of America, 1947-1959.

Mason, Bernard Sterling. **Woodcraft**. New York: A. S. Barnes, 1939.

Nessmuk (George W. Sears). **Woodcraft and Camping**. New York: Dover Publications, 1963.

Reynolds, E. E., editor. **B.P.'s Outlook Selections from Lord Baden Powell's contributions to The Scouter**. London: C. Arthur Pearson, 1941.

Schurz, Carl. Speech at Faneuil Hall, Boston, 1859.

Tagore, Rabindranath. **Fruit Gathering**. New York: Macmillan, 1916.

Thurman, John. **The Patrol Leaders' Handbook**. London: The Boy Scouts Association, 1950.

Wade, Eileen K. **27 Years with Baden-Powell**. London: Blandford Press, 1957.

The Paper Chase, Dir. James Bridges. Twentieth Century Fox, 1973.

Made in the USA
Charleston, SC
23 November 2013